Jeff en Mel

Thanks for -

Important Part of My Story.

May you Continue to Live

Beyond All Thinking

Jo Ann

You Are Special

Jeremiah 1: 5

BEYOND ALL THINKING

A Life of Purpose, Even after Seventy-Five

JoAnn Scoma McElroy

JoAnn Scoma McElroy

ISBN 978-1-0980-7953-6 (paperback)
ISBN 978-1-0980-8160-7 (hardcover)
ISBN 978-1-0980-7954-3 (digital)

Christian Faith Publishing, Inc.
832 Park Avenue
Meadville, PA 16335
www.christianfaithpublishing.com

Printed in the United States of America

INTRODUCTION

Why am I so nervous tonight? After all, I am a motivational speaker. The stage has never frightened me before. But tonight seems different.

My mentor Dr. Amy McNaughton, who helped me complete my dissertation in clinical counseling, is adjusting the collar of my graduation gown while I struggle to smooth the wrinkles on the front. It's almost time to leave the green room. We will take the long and anticipated walk across the stage together.

I adjust my cap one final time in the mirror and smile. This is my big moment, and I'm not going to miss a second of it.

Latecomers are settling into their pews near the back. The lights blind me, but the church appears to be full of people.

My high heels clip hollow against the wooden floor to the rhythm of my pounding heartbeat. Too much excitement. I summon an extra ounce of courage from Pastor Jeff, who's watching the countdown clock to begin this special occasion.

The dream of graduating with my classmates in Baton Rouge vanished when my husband's infirmity kept me in Pittsburgh. I couldn't march with my class as I'd hoped. But when Pastor Jeff heard of my dilemma, he and his staff quickly transformed the Saturday-night service into a graduation ceremony for one.

My time has finally arrived.

I've anticipated this night for years, envisioning my family and friends applauding and tooting their horns as I walk across the stage to receive my diploma. This isn't the big college auditorium of the college in Baton Rouge or the typical ceremony with its traditional pomp and circumstance. This is Allison Park Church.

These are the people who have come to share my special night with me.

I scan the audience from the wings, blinking my eyes to adjust to the bright lights. I search for my husband's wheelchair; it is usually at the back of the church, but it's nowhere to be seen.

Where is Hap? One would think after two marriages to the guy, I could find him tonight. His bipolar issues always leave room for concern. But God will see me through tonight.

Hap, with grandson Marty Jr., settling in for the graduation ceremony

Minutes before the ceremony begins, I spot Hap with his grandson Marty, who is here to assist him for the night. They are on their way down the aisle with the wheelchair, looking for a place close to the stage so Hap can witness the presentation.

I note Hap's stiff stature in the wheelchair, reminding me once again of his battle with Parkinson's—*our* battle with Parkinson's. The disease is a constant companion, coloring every day of our second marriage. This unyielding guest has overstayed his welcome, overwhelming both my husband and me as his caregiver, but tonight, Hap has come to share this moment with me.

The music is beginning—my cue to march out onto the stage. My hands tremble with excitement. I check my gown one last time. Although I'm anxious, I give a small salute to my clients and friends who are seated near the front. They are here to celebrate with me.

Once seated in my appointed spot, I catch a glimpse of Amy's smile of affirmation. Her steady encouragement has made this night possible. With the presentation in progress, Amy's voice echoes the same refrain, "You can do this," even when I was ready to give up.

In his resounding voice, Pastor Jeff lists my accomplishments, then describes the sacrifices I made to arrive at this moment. Long days and nights in the ER with Hap while preparing for an important exam the next day. Meeting with one client after another in my office. Grabbing another hour of study for my doctorate while managing a house with all its responsibilities. Then he mentions I will graduate *summa cum laude* tonight.

Pastor Jeff and Amy McNaughton at presentation of diploma

Oh my, the surprised expressions are heartwarming.

He closes by saying, "Oh, by the way, all this at the tender age of seventy-six." A shared gasp of disbelief is heard, and thunderous applause breaks out. Everyone is standing, clapping, and yelling, except for my husband in his wheelchair. He acknowledges his approval with a thumbs-up.

A smile of gratitude sweeps across my face. I can see through the bright lights now and recognize more of my clients and friends in the audience.

But wait, something is missing.

Missing!

Where are my children? I can't see them anywhere in these lights. I shield my eyes with my hand to scan the room. Ah, I spot two familiar faces in the back—Deanna and Dan. They're probably sitting back there to guard the food for the celebration after the ceremony.

I continue to search the crowd for other familiar faces. Where are my siblings? All seven of them? Maybe their invitations got lost in the mail. I am the matriarch of my family, and we always celebrate special occasions together.

Of course, Momma and Daddy are watching from above. I know how happy they must be for me at this moment. I can hear Daddy in his proud voice saying, *Way to go, sister. You have never let anything stop you from achieving your goals at any age.* I find solace in my hero's words.

I won't let their absence destroy my joy. Tonight, I'm ready to celebrate my doctorate degree, one I've worked hard to obtain in spite of all the hardships.

I remove my doctoral tam and wave to the audience as I leave the stage. The fleeting moments of disappointment fade with the thunderous applause from the audience. Those who are here tonight are here to celebrate this seventy-six-year-old overcoming all odds to reach her goal.

It is an evening to celebrate the possibilities *beyond all thinking—a life of purpose even after seventy-five.*

Lessons Learned

Sometimes disappointments have a way of merging despair into some of our greatest moments of accomplishments. Any form of rejection or disappointments, if not addressed promptly, can destroy all the good we've accomplished. Pain of resentment can move quickly into bitterness and anger, which can manifest later when we least expect it.

Resentment and bitterness, much like the venom of the poisonous snake, can kill if left unattended. A snake's bite can eventually destroy a life that once was healthy and vibrant.

I choose to march to the beat of winners and overcomers. Feelings of rejection and disappointments are just that.

Feelings.

Even though graduation night wasn't like I had hoped or dreamed, I accomplished a goal beyond my thinking.

A beautiful and elaborate celebration party was hosted by two of my children, Dan and Deanna, following the graduation ceremony.

I am quick to remind myself I am a winner.

I am not a victim tonight, I am a winner. I am better not bitter.

This is a test we will all face. We are not responsible for other people's choices, attitudes, or feelings.

How about you?

Are you a victor or victim?

What must you do to achieve your goals beyond your thinking?

Deanna, JoAnn, Dan

CHAPTER 1

Meet My Paternal Grandparents

He was only five-foot-eight, but this amazing man I called Daddy. Despite his stature, I saw him as a giant of a man—strong and caring.

Now settle in and let me introduce you to his parents and my grandparents. They fostered in my daddy determination from the time he was a child, and he did the same for me. Like my daddy, who was firstborn of six siblings, I too was firstborn of seven siblings.

With unwavering Sicilian tenacity, my grandparents made the long journey across the ocean to the USA despite many scary days and stormy nights. Their faces burst with pride and enthusiasm as they shared their Ellis Island venture from Corleone, Sicily, in 1910.

For a six-year-old, Sicily seemed so far away and 1910 so long ago. With my inquisitive young imagination, I asked Grandpa, Leo Luke Scoma, to tell me more.

"How big was the boat?"

"What did you eat?"

"Where did you sleep?"

As he continued bouncing me on his knee, my short little fingers reached toward his smiling face and tried to hold it still. Sometimes it was difficult to understand him when he spoke, and the bouncing was not helping. His Italian accent was so strong. If I could just clutch his mouth, I thought, he could talk better, and I could understand him. That didn't work either. However, my grandpa's smile was so big and kind I didn't need to understand all his words. The smile was enough.

Grandpa's hugs were robust, and I knew he loved me whenever he took time out from his busy life to tell me stories about when he was a little boy. After all, I was his first grandchild.

Grandpa was a shoemaker by trade in Corleone. He was twenty-five when he came to America. His first American shoe shop was in Richardson, Texas, near Dallas, until after the Depression.

Later, he opened a shop in Ennis, Texas. It was always crowded with anxious customers waiting their turn for Grandpa to say, "Can I hep a you?" He would carefully measure their feet for his custom-made shoes and scribble their name beside their order.

Daddy and Momma piled all eight of us kids in their 1945 Plymouth for the hour drive to Grandpa's shop almost every Saturday. We were his helpers for the day. There were not many modern conveniences at his shop, but he did have an indoor bathroom. He yelled something in Italian at us if we bothered his leathers or his hammers. We didn't understand Italian, but we did understand his tone when we did something wrong.

The smell of new and old leather permeated his small shop and traveled all the way to the sidewalk.

And so did the burnt coffee.

He was an excellent shoemaker and repairer; Grandpa could create or repair anything of leather. When he finished a repair, the shoes looked brand-new. There was always a look of disbelief when he handed them back to his grateful customers.

My grandpa became a successful businessman. There were no opening or closing hours at his shop. If customers were there, he worked until the last person left. To me, this industrious little man, whose smile could light up the entire town, was my grandpa, who talked funny.

Josephine Salerno, my grandma, was known as Josie to her friends and family. The Jo of my name came from Josephine. Less than five feet tall and feisty, she was as hard to understand as my grandpa. Everybody loved my grandma.

She was only fourteen when her parents brought her with her four siblings to America. I had many questions for her.

"Grandma, how did you meet Grandpa?"

Her broad smile assured me she was delighted to tell her story to me. Hers also came with a mixture of Italian and butchered English.

She was only sixteen, and Grandpa twenty-seven, when they began an arranged courtship. Hesitant and unready for marriage at sixteen, she later consented after constant coercion from her father.

"What's an arranged marriage?" I asked.

Grandma explained it was the Italian custom at that time. She and Grandpa had only seen each other at mass on Sundays but had never spoken to each other. Later after meeting each other at a cousin's house several times, Grandma's father told her that my grandpa wanted to marry her. "I didn't want to get married," she said, "but I finally said yes."

I didn't understand this. "Why?"

She lifted a shoulder. "It was what my father wanted."

She explained how she and Grandpa were never allowed to be left alone. If they went to a movie, the entire family would go. Her mother would sit by her, and Grandpa's father would sit beside him.

With a sigh, she described how the date for her marriage was finally set for June 17, 1912. "I did not look forward to this. I was so young, and he was a lot older. But it would be a big date for us," Grandma said. "But it also meant Grandpa was allowed to come to my house to court me." She played with her long black braid as she spoke, her glasses halfway down her nose.

"What does 'court' mean, Grandma?" I asked.

Grandma's voice raised an octave. "It meant that Grandpa visited often. Still we weren't allowed to be alone. And that was fine with me." Sitting in her favorite creaking rocking chair, she continued, "The days and weeks seemed to move too swiftly. I was just a frightened teenage girl about to be married. I didn't really know what love was."

"What was your wedding like?"

Josie and Luke, Wedding Day, June 1912

"I remember it like it was yesterday. It was a traditional Catholic wedding. Of course, all the family members were there. They were all seated in their proper pews to witness this marriage that had been so closely guarded."

"What happened then, Grandma?" I was mesmerized by the details.

"Well, Grandpa was now permitted to be with me in our rented house in Dallas. And we were finally allowed time alone together on the porch swing." She chuckled. "Even though we were married, we were still under the watchful eyes of our families."

"Did you ever get to go inside the house together?" I asked.

"In time, dear. And two years later, your daddy, Louis, was born on July 24, 1914. Six more children followed. These were your aunts and uncle."

"And Daddy's youngest sister, Elizabeth, was born one year after I was born, right?"

"Yes, when Elizabeth was born, I was thirty-nine and you were one year old—my very first grandchild."

It didn't make a lot of sense to me. Elizabeth was my aunt Liz, but we grew up as though we were sisters. We played together, shared childhood dreams, and later big-girl goals.

Because we were so close in age, we spent most days and nights together. My mother—Annie to Liz—always did a great job of meeting both our girlish needs. Whenever Lizzy wanted her very coarse, straight hair to look like my curls, she'd ask Annie to braid her hair. When Momma took the braids out, her hair was wavy. She was so proud.

Elizabeth called my father Louie, but I called him Daddy. It was a little challenging from time to time for him. Liz was his baby sister, not his daughter. But both my parents treated us like equals.

Modern technology replaced the old-fashioned era of my grandparents from Italy, yet many memories remain of my grandparents, and they have had a vivid impact on my early life.

Memories of their Love Field home are countless. The old ice truck delivering their ice once a week. The driver responding to the card in the window. He knew how much ice was needed for that day's visit: *twenty-five* or *fifty pounds*.

Perched on the kitchen window, I watched the driver as he left his truck. Running to the back porch to meet him, I unlocked the screen door for him to make his delivery.

After he slipped the leather vest over his back and yanked huge tongs out of the back of his truck, I opened the door so he could deliver the requested amount of ice.

My job was to open the icebox door for him after he chipped the ice to fit the block into the wooden icebox. I stood close by and had to cover my face to protect my eyes from the flying ice chips until the door would close.

Oh my goodness. I cannot forget Grandpa's orchards.

What a proud accomplishment of his. He was so proud of the different fruit trees and his vineyards. Grandpa was passionate about his cherry, peach, and apricot trees. But his amazing grape vineyards were his pride and joy. From those vineyards, he produced his fine wines, or so he thought.

It was customary on Sunday after church for our family to eat lunch at my grandparents' home. The traditional Italian meal was spaghetti and meatballs and fried chicken, prepared by Grandma. This was usually served with either green beans or green peas. The smell of garlic, fried chicken, and fresh baked bread met our senses when we walked through the kitchen door. It was overwhelming, and we were starving.

Their big dining room was where it all happened. The windows were opened, and those ugly yellow curtains swirled in the gentle breezes behind the table filled with food. This room was always filled with an abundance of noisy laughter. The smell of *sugo*, also known as sauce or gravy for our spaghetti, beckoned us to find our seats at the table.

After everyone was seated around the extended, long brown oak table, Daddy prayed the blessing. Afterward, Grandpa would stand and serve everyone from the stack of plates in front of him. In his heavy dialect he would say, "How-a much-a you-a want-a?" After he filled the plate, he poured a generous amount of *sugo* over the pasta. A large meatball plopped on top completed the serving.

After everyone had their plates in front of them, Grandma would come around to the children first with a huge platter of fried chicken and ask, "White-ta or dark-a?" If anyone wanted some freshly grated Parmesan cheese over their pasta, Grandpa would do the honors.

But Grandpa always liked to fill his plate first before he served anyone else. He would set aside his generously rounded-up portion of pasta, topped with the *sugo* and freshly grated Parmesan cheese. Two perfectly round meatballs on the side of his plate completed his stash.

Why?

I am not sure why.

There were twelve of us seated around the table after Grandma had securely positioned her old ironing board across two chairs to seat more people. The smallest kids got to sit on the ironing board seat. It was important that all of us be seated at the same table. This was family time.

However, our Italian family continued to grow. Grandma eventually had to set up another table in the kitchen—the kids' table. Most of the time, I got to sit at the grown-ups' table since I was the oldest.

On a typical Sunday afternoon, the grown-ups would retire to the porch swings and hammock to talk. That was when the older kids went out to play in the orchard and the younger ones stayed with Momma. My brother Lou, aka Sonny, had a fun game for us big kids. It was called Let's Go Exploring.

Grandpa had given us strict orders many times never to go anywhere near his wine cellar. So his wine cellar became a tantalizing mystery to us kids.

"Why can't we see the wine cellar?"

Grandpa never said why.

Maybe it was because the cellar was at the bottom of the old well, accessible only by a long rope and a wooden ladder. Grandpa dug this well, and the water piped from it into the family house and the six rental houses on his two acres. The well never ran dry.

Of course, my brother's idea of exploring sounded like fun. The oldest of my siblings and cousins, I was usually the one in charge, but not today—Sonny was our leader.

It took three of us to lift the huge metal door that covered the well.

Who would descend first? The rope and wooden ladder looked intimidating to us, but adventure, here we come!

I was the first one. I had to be brave for the remaining five. The ladder swayed gently, but I gripped the rope so tightly I got blisters on my hands. Each one took turns descending the ladder into the well, and I greeted them as they landed. Sonny made sure everyone got down okay, and I made sure everyone landed okay.

My eyes stayed focused on our leader, Sonny. My mind raced. *It is so dark and scary.*

Of course the purpose of our adventure was to find and taste the wine. With the little tasting cups that were there, we each sampled a little from the closest barrel, and I do mean we took just a little sip of the grape wine.

We found out quickly: fermenting wine is not a good thing to drink. Very quickly we were ready to go back to familiar territory—the orchard and daylight.

It was harder to climb back up a dangling ladder on the inside of a dark well than it was to go down. Especially challenging when we weren't feeling so well. One by one, we struggled back up the ladder to safe and firm ground. I'm not sure how firm we were. Feeling so sick and scared, each one found a tree in the orchard to lie under out of the sun…and die.

It wasn't long before the adults became concerned about the kids. We were too quiet. They immediately began their search for us.

Grandma with her apron still around her neck, Grandpa with his buttoned-up shirt tucked inside his pants supported by his suspenders. Our parents were walking through the orchard, calling us by name. Momma with a baby in her arms and Daddy still in his Sunday clothes without his necktie looked overly concerned.

We were too sick to answer roll call. Life looked dismal.

With his sharp eye, Grandpa spotted us, sick and crying under his cherry trees. We knew we were in *big* trouble. Grandpa ambled up to each of us as we were lying under the trees longing to die. He glared at us, his hands pressed to his hips, his glasses on top of his head. Then he said something in Italian. I am not sure what he said, but I don't think it was for us to understand.

What we did understand when his Italian temper cooled off was a "blessing" in his broken English.

"I tell a you a once, I tell a you a twice, no touch a my wine. I pray a to God you a die." That was not the kind of blessing we wanted from our grandpa as our last rites.

Lesson Learned

Do not follow the leader down into the well and drink fermented wine. It can be dark, cold, and scary. It's not worth the nasty taste or Grandpa's *blessing*.

Christmas Traditions

Christmases were always special at Grandma and Grandpa's house, especially on Christmas Eve. The fragrance of the freshly cut tree decorated with fresh pine cones was overwhelming. Presents that we'd shaken and tried peeking into were stacked high all around the tree in the living room. We would be opening these presents before we left to go to our house to wait for Santa to come later that night.

Aww, can you smell the distinct traditional aroma of the *sfincione*? This Sicilian fish pizza aroma filled every room of the house. It took a while to acquire a love and taste for this pizza, which is usually served as a traditional holiday snack. I always thought the anchovies smelled more like dirty socks. Ugh!

Grandma always made sure to make plain *sfincione* for all us kids, and some adults too without the anchovies. *Sfincione* is one of the most traditional Sicilian pizzas that originated in the Palermo area, where my grandparents migrated from. Grandma used to make it just for Christmas, but then it became a tradition as well on New Year's Day for good luck.

Grandpa and I would take long, relaxing strolls at the market in search for the exact "just right cheeses." He was very particular about his cheeses. The tomatoes for the sauce were also critical, as were the anchovies. The additional extra-virgin olive oil, in its huge green glass bottle, was used to dribble over the top. That was my favorite part of this tradition. I got to help Grandma drizzle the olive oil over the dough. I later developed a love for the taste of *sfincione*, pronounced [fin juney] as I got older.

Returning home in our cramped four-door Plymouth, our voices became louder and higher pitched with anticipation of Santa's arrival. We knew we would have to wait until Christmas morning to see if Santa thought we had been good or bad. Most often, he left us what we had wished for. I didn't know how he managed to grant so many wishes for so many people.

I couldn't understand why Grandma didn't want us to believe in Santa. Poor Grandma, she just didn't get it. She even told Liz there was no Santa.

This really confused her because my daddy, her brother, told her there was a Santa. Liz chose to hang with us at Christmas. She received more gifts if she believed.

I was thirteen years old before I knew the truth about Santa. I think I still believe in him today. He's such a nice old jolly man. He likes making people happy, so how can that be so bad?

What do all my childhood memories have to do with my story?

I believe that my behavior and personality traits are extensions of my childhood experiences.

Researchers have found that people who had good childhood memories of their parental relationships tend to have better health, less depression, and fewer chronic illnesses as older adults.

The most surprising finding in a study conducted by the American Psychological Association was that the effects did not fade over time, but positive childhood memories still predicted better physical and mental health when people were in middle age and older adulthood.

Memories of the old kerosene heaters and wood-burning kitchen stove.

The brown wooden icebox that sat in the corner of the kitchen all alone with an embroidered cloth hanging down over the top.

The water well that supplied the cold, tasty water electrically, sometimes had to be pumped by hand whenever the power failed. It also served as a storage for Grandpa's wines.

For these positive memories, I am most grateful.

I don't think my grandparents would appreciate or understand all our modern conveniences today. They would say everything goes too fast. And fast can't be good for us.

Other early childhood memories, which have become my legacy, are my grandparents' and parents' accomplishments and the satisfaction they derived from them.

Struggle was part of their inherent personalities.

This is one of the stories my grandma told me of Grandpa's ice cream cart before I was born:

"What's the hurry?" Grandpa would say while strolling up and down the neighborhood streets, pushing his little ice cream cart. His handheld bell rang continuously, announcing his arrival.

Then came the children, running and clutching their money tightly in their little sweaty hands. They were yelling "wait" from all directions. Grandpa would park his cart on the side of the road—stoop down and give lots of hugs with the ice cream purchases. He was patient and even helped the little ones remove the wrappers from their favorite ice cream.

Grandpa's Ice Cream Bell

Grandpa's old hand bell resides on my shelf to admire, and from time to time, I ring it just to remember my grandpa with his ice cream cart.

No car for my grandpa! My little five-foot-five grandfather chose to ride his bicycle rather than drive a car. Even though he was hit twice while riding his bike to work in Ennis, Texas, he thought it was much safer than a car. He never owned or drove an automobile but didn't mind riding in one.

Grandpa Luke and Grandma Josie lived and enjoyed their lives as citizens of America with their seven children and the many grand- and great-grandchildren.

The Legacy

Grandpa suffered from several heart attacks, his first one when he was fifty-seven. When he was seventy-two, it was fatal. Grandpa was buried in Dallas in our Scoma family plot and will always be remembered by his granddaughter—his first grandchild—for his big smile, bad wine, and funny accent.

Grandma continued to live a busy life, preaching and travelling, sharing her story of conversion from the Catholic Church. She had a big impact on my ministry when I was not old enough to drive. She played a vital role in the Scoma girls' evangelistic team. She was our chauffeur and shared her testimony in our revivals.

Grandma and Grandpa's first great grandchildren, Danny and Debbie

My grandma Josie died when she was two days short of her eighty-third birthday. She too was buried in our family plot in Dallas.

What about you?

1. What memories do you have of your grandparents?
2. What is their legacy they left for you?
3. What behavior and personality traits did you inherit from them?
4. What legacy can you leave for your family?

CHAPTER 2

I was known before I was born

Mamma and daddy with their 8 children

Before I formed you in the womb, I knew you,
before you were born I set you apart;

—Jeremiah 1:5 NIV

It was 1935 near the end of the Great Depression. My Italian parents, Louis Scoma and Annie Digiglio Scoma, celebrated the birth of their first child at St. Paul Hospital in Dallas, Texas. My young parents were anxious to bring me home under the guiding eye of my mothers' mother, whom I called Mamo. My mother was one of thirteen children, so Mamo was well experienced. My young mother welcomed the daily help from her in learning the basics of motherhood.

I was named Jo Ann from a combination of my paternal grandmother, Josephine, and Annie, my mother.

I must have been around six years old when I first heard my aunts and uncles sitting around our dining room table talking about the Depression days. Intrigued by their conversation, I asked, "What is a depression?"

"We'll talk about it tomorrow," Daddy said.

The next day, after the dinner dishes were washed and put away, my parents seated themselves across from me at our yellow chrome kitchen table.

Daddy asked, "Would you like to know what life was like for us before you were born?"

I nodded, always curious about my family.

"It was the worst economic time in history."

"What's economic," I asked.

"There was no money or food. Many families suffered through it. It lasted from 1929 to 1939. Your mother and I were married in 1934 right in the middle of the Depression. Banks closed, causing millions of families to lose their savings. Many were unable to pay their bills or rent payments, so they were kicked out of their homes. Momma was concerned about the children who went to bed hungry and didn't have enough warm clothes to wear.

"That must have been terrible," I said.

"It was tough for us as a young couple. Starting a family could be a challenge when there's no money," Momma said. "But Daddy was convinced that his family-to-be would not become a statistic. He explained that men were expected to be the breadwinners of their families."

My little six-year-old body was getting tired, but I wanted to hear the rest of my parents' story. So after sitting for a good while, I asked to be excused to the bathroom and to get a drink of water. I hurried back to hear more of their story.

After I settled back in my chair, Daddy continued, "Many of our friends couldn't find jobs. They were unable to provide for their families, and this made them feel like failures." Daddy looked away for a few minutes, and to my six-year-old eyes, he looked sad. "Some of these men deserted their families altogether."

"What does deserted mean?"

"They just left and never came back. Like some of your uncles, many of them began drinking."

"But you didn't do that."

"No, your momma and I will never leave you. We want you to have a normal life with no worries about money or food."

"Does this help you understand the Depression days?"

"Yes, it does, and I'm happy you are my momma and daddy."

Momma and Daddy exceeded their determination to maintain a normal life for their family. With my three brothers, we each had daily chores to do. When I was eight, my brother Sonny was six, Charles four, and Baby Lawrence two.

The only girl and firstborn, I was expected to be the biggest helper to my mother.

Our beds must be made before we could leave our room for breakfast, but Baby Lawrence got a pass.

For family entertainment, we gathered around the radio in our living room in our specific chairs. We listened intently to storytellers and mystery shows. Sometimes we had to wait until the static stopped to hear the end of the story.

Monopoly became a family favorite even though it took forever to finish a game. Daddy had to explain the rules over and over to the younger ones.

Family devotion time was also important. Each of us took our turn reading from the Bible. The older children assisted the younger ones. We did most everything together as a family.

My parents' young family soon grew to a total of five boys and three girls. The first five were Sonny, Charles, Lawrence, Lillian, and me. A teenager when the final three arrived, I was valuable help for my momma. Samuel Ray and Stephen Ray were eleven months apart, and Camellia Ruth, the baby and caboose, was eighteen months old when I married. I was her second momma from the day she was born. This was one big Protestant Italian family.

Known before I Was Born

It was a traditional Sunday after church at Grandma's house—pasta, fried chicken, and banana pudding. But today was different. After the meal, Daddy invited me to come and sit beside him in the big swing on the porch. This was where the adults would gather to talk after lunch.

The familiar squeak of the swing could be heard throughout the house and backyard. A soft and gentle Texas breeze was pushing the swing when I ran out on the porch.

I positioned myself, my legs dangling. A soft streak of sunshine swept across my face and through my curly brown hair.

Daddy stopped swinging, and so did the familiar squeak.

I became curious when his face became serious. He looked straight into my eyes and cleared his throat. Not sure of what I'd done, I fidgeted.

"Nothing to worry about," he said, detecting the worry on my face. "I just wanted to express how proud I am that you became a newborn Christian."

Just the week before, I'd asked Jesus to come into my heart as my Lord and Savior. It had been a special Sunday morning, February 7, 1945, at Lisbon Assembly of God Church in Dallas, Texas. I was ten years old when I accepted Jesus as my Lord and Savior.

"Do you want to know why I asked you to join me on the swing?" Daddy asked.

I nodded, feeling important and proud.

"I have something important to tell you. Something I never want you to forget. Before you were born, God told me about you. He told me you would be chosen and anointed by him to be part of a ministry."

Wow, this was exciting to hear, but when would this happen? I was only ten years old. How would I know when it was time for me to experience what God had told my daddy?

Before I formed thee in the belly I knew
thee; and before thou camest forth out of the

> womb I sanctified thee, *and* I ordained thee a
> prophet unto the nations. (Jeremiah 1:5 KJV)

Looking back, God began preparing me for ministry as a young student at Boude Storey Middle School and Adamson High School. Two strategic and powerful teachers played a dominant role of influence in my life.

First, I must introduce Ms. Beulah Brown.

I was twelve years old, four-foot-eleven, and at first, I was scared of the teacher. A quick glimpse at Ms. Beulah Brown and you too would find her an intimidating woman. At the time, I didn't value her wisdom or the love she showed each of her students; however, today she is my heroine.

Ms. Beulah—that was what she wanted us to call her—was tall and stout. Her long black hair with scattered specks of grey was pulled tight in a bun on top of her head. This was also where Ms. Beulah wore the glasses she was always searching for. Her black dress, the only color she ever wore, almost reached her black lace-up shoes.

Ms. Beulah's hugs were amazing. She smothered me into her huge bosom for the best hugs. She always made me feel special. Almost every day she reminded us students she was never too busy to talk and pray with us, anytime we needed her. And she made sure we knew that Jesus was our best friend.

The one requirement she insisted on was we had to learn 1 Corinthians 10:13. Not just learn it but know it and write it. One-third of our final grade depended on writing it correctly. By correctly, she meant every comma, period, and semicolon in its correct place. I learned it, still quote it, and live by it today. Thank you, Ms. Beulah Brown, for your legacy.

> There hath no temptation taken you but
> such as is common to man: but God is faithful,
> who will not suffer you to be tempted above that
> which you are able; but will with the temptation
> also make a way to escape, that ye may be able to
> bear it. (1 Corinthians 10:13)

I now present Mr. Carl Nutley, my hero.

Other than my salvation, Mr. Carl Nutley was the greatest life changer in my young life.

I was a fourteen-year-old high school freshman. My adviser informed me I needed an additional credit course for the semester. There were no options available except for one. Mr. Nutley's public speaking and debate class had an opening that would work with my schedule.

Extremely shy, I was scared of the word *public* In groups I kept to myself. From the description of this class, I wanted absolutely nothing to do with it. Yet I was told it was my only option. Reluctantly, I went to his class with a teacher escort.

As soon as I walked into his classroom, I immediately knew it was not going to work.

The class was already in session. Mr. Nutley was seated in the back of the room checking roll when I walked in.

Standing in front of the class, not knowing where to sit, I froze when Mr. Nutley's loud voice addressed me: "Name, please?"

"Jo Ann Scoma," I muttered.

It wasn't loud enough for him, so again in his loud voice, he said, "Name, please?"

Aware of everyone's eyes glaring at me, I spoke in a voice that was an octave higher but not much louder, "Jo Ann Scoma."

The situation was growing disturbing. I was ready to bail when once again, Mr. Nutley thumped his pencil on his desk asked in a stern voice, "Name, please?"

At this stage of the battle of wills, in my not-so-quiet voice, I yelled back, "Jo Ann Scoma, and I'm getting out of this class."

Mr. Nutley must not have understood me because in a nicer voice, he said, "Take a seat please."

Did he say take a seat? Doesn't he know how angry I am? Where is a seat? Forget how embarrassed I was, standing in front of twenty-five giggling classmates.

Anxiously, I watched the clock on his desk, waiting for the bell to ring. Seconds after it did, I headed to the counselor's office. Not good. There were no other options.

For three years I remained in Mr. Nutley's classes. His tenacity and commitment toward me was *beyond all thinking*.

As a result of Mr. Nutley's guidance and patience, my colleague Cheree Hughes and I won a state championship in one of our debate competitions. No longer frightened by standing in front of an audience, I became an accomplished speaker. I looked forward to each new challenge and debate competition.

Overcoming the number one fear of speaking in front of an audience can make one confident for other challenges in life. When someone else believes in us, it's much easier to believe in ourselves. It happened when I was sixteen, just before graduation. Mr. Nutley called me to his classroom. Nervous and concerned, I waited outside. What had I done?

"Yes, sir?" I took a seat in front of him.

He smiled. "I want to tell you after all these years why I invested so much time and energy in you."

I squirmed and peered up.

"The early-morning and after-school sessions were not just to prepare you for upcoming events but for a lifetime of events. Do you remember that first day when you came into my class?"

I gulped and nodded. "I did not want to be there."

"I saw a scared and confused little girl. You were unsure, frightened, and angry, and that's what it takes to be an overcomer of life's uncertainties. It takes these traits to develop quality speakers.

I frowned. "They don't sound like qualities of a good speaker."

"I saw in you a beautiful butterfly still in the cocoon, but there was no doubt a beautiful butterfly waiting to spread her wings."

I left that meeting with Mr. Nutley a determined girl, unlike the scared little fourteen-year-old girl of years earlier. A butterfly—I liked that.

Lesson Learned

To schoolteachers everywhere reading my story, please don't think of yourself as just a teacher. You are the Ms. Beulahs and Mr. Nutleys of this generation, pouring into our children's, grandchildren's, and great-grandchildren's futures. We honor you today as champions of our generation.

It's your turn now.

1. Can you remember a teacher or teachers who influenced your life choices?
2. If they are still alive, would you honor them in some way?

Dedicated to You, Mr. Nutley: An Excerpt from My Dissertation

A butterfly goes through stages of transformation before it can emerge and share its beauty. Eventually the effect of the butterfly's journey allows it to climb free and rest. Spreading its wings for the first time, energy flows through them and they expand, finally ready to carry the butterfly on the breeze. We too will feel confident with our new self. Like the butterfly we can flutter about to new and exciting heights.

A Teenager in God's Time

Before you were born, I set you apart; I ordained (appointed) you as a prophet. The Lord put forth his hand and touched my mouth and said, "Behold I have put my words in your mouth." (Jeremiah 1:5)

I was a sophomore when I was called to the guidance counselor's office.

It was a sunny Monday morning, but I was a little nervous. After I was seated in front of his desk, he glanced at my shaking hands and calmly asked if I would like to graduate a year earlier with the class of 1952. He explained that I had acquired enough credits and qualified for early graduation. He went on to warn me that I would not be graduating with my familiar classmates.

This was too big a decision for me to make alone to not graduate with my classmates. I asked if I could discuss this with my parents and give him an answer later. He agreed.

That evening, my parents and I discussed the pros and cons of this choice. After praying, we decided I would graduate with the class of 1952 as a sixteen-year-old graduate.

A Sunday That Changed My Destiny

It was a special Sunday morning designated to honor and celebrate all the high school graduates of Oak Cliff Assembly of God Church. My pastor, Brother H. C. Noah, reserved the front-row seating for all the honorees.

At the beginning of his sermon, he addressed us specifically as young adults. He wanted each of us to know the urgent purpose of this day and his sermon. We were at the crossroads of our lives and would be making many lifelong decisions. He emphasized how those decisions would affect the rest of our lives. This decision I would have to make on my own, without my parents' help.

At the conclusion of his sermon, he appealed to each graduate to come forward and stand for a prayer of blessing.

When he concluded his blessing, he solemnly invited each of us to go into one of the nearby prayer rooms. With much passion in his appeal, he asked us not to leave the prayer room until we knew for sure what God's plan was for our lives.

Sometime later, Daddy stopped by the room where I was praying. He gently asked if I was ready to go home.

I was not ready.

I did not know when I would be ready.

We agreed I would call as soon as I received my assignment from God. Everyone else had left except for me, but I had to know God's assignment. He had already spoken to my daddy before I was born and told him I was going be used for his kingdom's work.

It was late, and evening was fast approaching. The church would soon be active again with the evening service. Alone in the prayer room, I still waited to hear my direction from God.

Then it happened.

I experienced two unbelievable encounters in my prayer-room vigil.

While I was standing in the middle of the room, something amazing was happening. I found myself standing in a huge field of wheat. The wheat had already been partially gleaned from a recent harvest, and the rest was lying in the field.

I was strolling slowly with my hands behind my back among the rows when, suddenly, my foot struck a metal object covered with fallen wheat. With my limited knowledge regarding farming or its equipment, I immediately stopped to investigate the unfamiliar object.

My most vivid recollection of farming was on our family's yearly vacation to Aunt Pauline's farm in Houston, Texas. She would let us gather eggs, help milk cows, and feed the hogs. I didn't remember ever seeing an object like this before on her farm.

Curious, I stooped down and brushed the wheat aside. Struggling, I tried to pick it up, but it was much too heavy for me alone. Still trying to identify this strangely shaped piece of metal, I heard footsteps approaching me, but I was so preoccupied with the curious object at first I didn't acknowledge the visitor approaching. Then I thought the approaching visitor might own the field. He would know what this weird semicircular metal object with its short wooden handle was used for. The blade looked sharp, and it was obvious it had been used to harvest the fallen wheat.

Soon the footsteps stopped directly in front of my stooped body. The man must have noticed my struggle because he asked, "Can I help you?"

I immediately answered, "Yes please, this thing is so heavy, and I can't lift it. I'm not sure what it is."

He lowered himself to the ground to help but didn't say anything.

I asked again, "What is this thing for? It's so heavy, and I can't lift it."

"It's a sickle," he answered. With the sickle still in my hands, he placed his hands over mine and said, "Together we will glean the field."

It was at that moment I immediately noticed the scars on his hands.

It was Jesus!

Trembling now, I realized I was talking with Jesus.

After we both stood, he strolled with me through the field. He spoke with such authority, "The Holy Spirit will be your teacher and instructor, and he will teach you all things. He will show you how to harvest the field with great results."

Wow, what a challenge!

We were still walking together as he continued to show me how to use the sickle. His hands firmly gripping mine, he showed me how to harvest wheat. That was when I noticed his sandals and scarred feet.

Words cannot describe the feelings that overwhelmed me with this amazing visit with Jesus. I was beyond honored and excited. The master teacher himself taught me. What he taught me in that short period of time was my confirmation. I was born to harvest souls for the kingdom. The harvest was ripe and ready to be gleaned.

We stopped walking. I laid the sickle down.

But just as quickly and quietly as he had appeared, he left. I wanted to thank him for the lessons he taught me that day. It was an experience that changed my life forever.

Soon after the amazing encounter with Jesus, and much later in the evening, I had a not-so-pleasant experience.

God permitted me a close-up view of what hell was like.

He wanted me to warn people about hell. As my teacher, he thought I should have a virtual experience.

The same room where I had experienced the sickle and harvest field was transformed into another unbelievable experience. Standing in the center of the room, I saw something moving toward me. At first glance, it looked like huge ocean waves. As the waves moved closer to where I was standing, I realized this was not water but liquid flames. As they continued rolling closer toward me, the heat became intense.

The sight I saw was the most terrifying picture of humanity I'd ever seen. Men and women were screaming while pulling at their hair. Their excruciating pain caused some to bite the people who were closest to them. Their faces showed fear and immense pain. They pleaded for someone to please help.

Unsure of what to do, I moved a little closer to offer help. I wanted to rescue them from their torment.

The flames were steadily rolling closer to me and hindered me from reaching them. There seemed to be a transparent wall that separated them from me. My heart ached from pounding so hard. The profound pain and the sense of their helplessness was indescribable. As desperate as I was to help them, there was nothing I could do.

From the intensity of the flames and heat, my entire body was dripping wet. I became nauseous from the smell of burning flesh that was not being consumed. The magnitude of their screams was deafening.

But what I saw next brought me to my knees weeping. I saw a relative of mine being swept toward me in a hurling wave of flames. I quickly reached to take hold of his hand, but the wall separated us.

He pled with me in his heavy Italian accent, "Go, a tell-a my people no come-a here. It's a bad-a place. I hurt." In a flash, he too was swept away by another wave. There was nothing I could do to help those terrified people.

But God wanted to show me how I could help others. I could help by warning men and women that hell is real. I could help them to prepare to see Jesus and not experience hell.

It was late well into the night before my prayer-room experience ended. Physically, I was exhausted, and yet I was in awe of what I experienced in that prayer room. That day was life changing forever.

Daddy had been anticipating my phone call and was there in fifteen minutes to take me home. I left the prayer room that night a changed teenage girl with so much wonder and excitement for my new assignment to come.

When would this assignment begin? How could I accomplish such an awesome responsibility? I was so grateful my pastor insisted we stay until we received our assignment from God.

Without a doubt, I knew God would open doors of opportunity for me soon. He had chosen me. It was going to be an unbelievable journey.

I didn't share my prayer-room encounters with anyone for quite some time, not even with my parents. It was still an unbelievable experience I had just encountered and so much to contemplate.

Why was I called to such a high calling? I am still not sure. Still in awe from my prayer-room experiences, I made an agreement with God. I chose not to let anyone know about the experiences I had encountered. I asked him, when the time was right, if he would have a pastor contact me to come and preach.

The only seminary training I had before standing behind a pulpit for the first time was from Jesus himself. I soon became a student of the Word and began preparing for my assignment. I didn't know when the call would come for me to minister, but I knew it would be soon.

Six months later, it happened.

Early Monday morning, while I was getting ready to leave for work, our phone rang. Daddy answered the phone. I could tell by his voice he was a little hesitant in his conversation.

"Yes…yes…okay…hold, please. I will get her to the phone."

I made my way down the narrow hallway to answer this mysterious phone call. Daddy handed me the yellow receiver that hung on the wall in our kitchen. The puzzled look on his face made me curious. Who could possibly be calling me at seven o'clock on a Monday morning?

"Hello," I said in my not-so-confident voice.

"Sister Jo Ann, this is Brother Mangrum. I am calling to ask you to come and preach at my church this Wednesday night."

I chuckled and assured him he was calling the wrong person. "I am sure you want my grandmother. She is a licensed minister with the Assemblies of God."

Brother Mangrum was the presbyter of the Dallas area churches. Our conversation continued.

"No, Sister Jo Ann, I know your grandmother, but this morning God was very specific for me to call you."

I immediately responded, "Did you say God told you to call me?"

Then I remembered my agreement with God six months before. Without another moment's hesitation, I said, "Where's your church?"

When that phone call ended, my calling and journey began.

Since I wasn't old enough to drive yet, my parents had to drive me Wednesday evening to Arcadia Park Assembly of God Church in Dallas. When Daddy pulled up in front of the church, I felt butterflies in my tummy. In Texas we would say, "I was downright nervous."

The congregation had no idea this was going to be my first sermon or how frightened I was. What if I got diarrhea from all my nervousness?

After Brother Mangrum completed his introduction, I found myself peeking over a pulpit for the first time, scared and nervous. The eyes of the audience stared back at me with expectation, some with curiosity.

Would God stand beside me even now and fulfill the promises of my recent encounters with him?

What would the congregation expect from a sixteen-year-old girl just recently called to preach?

The same feelings I felt when I first walked into Mr. Carl Nutley's public speaking classroom was what I felt that night.

I wanted out.

Then I remembered a king in the Bible named Belshazzar. He saw the hand of God writing on the wall of his palace. His knees shook one against the other from his fear of God.

I did not see a hand writing on the wall of the church, but what I did see was the hand of God that had positioned me on this platform for his purpose. My knees, like Belshazzar's, knocked against one another as I tightly gripped the pulpit. I was nervous.

Then it all changed.

Confidence and strength enveloped me as I began to preach. The words flowed with power and anointing. My sermon was from Luke 14:23, and I challenged the people to step outside their comfort zones. At the close of my sermon, I invited everyone to accept Jesus as their Lord and Savior if they did not know him. The response was overwhelming, and my spirit was overjoyed. Many healing miracles also occurred that night.

In response to my sermon, with new zeal and determination, the congregation continued with their building program. They began to knock on doors and invite people to come to church. Soon the church's membership and attendance grew to an amazing high point. The grateful congregation enjoyed their new much larger facilities.

News about the teenage preacher girl raised some eyebrows and much curiosity. Excitement swept swiftly across the Dallas area churches. Pastors called to see when I would be available to speak at their churches. God was certainly busy keeping his end of our agreement.

None were calling for a single service; they were interested in a revival.

Brother Roy Sparks, pastor of the Bluebonnet Assembly of God, gave me the first revival invitation, and I accepted.

Revivals require more than three sermons in one's preaching arsenal. It requires two weeks or more of sermons.

This could be a big problem.

With only three sermons, how could I preach a revival? This didn't seem to be the only dilemma facing me. Brother Sparks wanted me to agree to begin in two weeks so he could start advertising immediately.

I was sure Brother Sparks, a pastor for many years, would certainly understand I would need more time to prepare additional sermons for a revival. And this would give him more time for advertising.

"No way," was his response. "Preach the three sermons, and if God doesn't give you more, preach them over again."

I agreed.

Still, I needed to write more. A sermon was not a written essay; it was preparing a message under the leadership of the Holy Spirit.

Brochures were printed and distributed. Newspaper announcements were published. The revival was fast approaching, and all I had were my three sermons and I was working on another, but my full-time job at Sears didn't give me much time for preparation of the sermons.

The Bluebonnet revival began in early April on a Sunday evening. Young and old came to see and hear the young preacher girl.

God's amazing blessings were manifested nightly in the revival. I preached, sang, and prayed for people who were sick or in need of salvation. Just as predicted by Brother Sparks, the revival continued for three weeks. No sermon was repeated.

I was amazed and humbled by the overflowing crowds and their enormous enthusiasm each evening. Every seat was taken by old and young alike. They were all eager to hear the young girl play her accordion, sing, and preach.

I did not anticipate such a response with my lack of experience. The lesson I learned from this experience: if God asks us to do something, he will provide all the necessary ingredients to accomplish something good.

The response to the altar for salvation each evening was overwhelming. There were unbelievable, miraculous healings from many illnesses. The Bluebonnet revival remains as one of my fondest memories. Although it was my first revival, God was in charge, and the glory and honor were all his.

Faster than the speed of light, results from this revival spread quickly across the Dallas area. Many pastors I didn't know were there each evening to witness this teenage girl evangelist. They too were amazed at what they experienced. The calendar began to fill up quickly.

An invitation for another revival was extended from Pastor Stephen Oates. His opening date: "as soon as this one closes." His church, Love Field Assembly of God was also in Dallas, the church where my grandmother attended and testified about her conversion.

Feeling a little more confident, I said yes for this revival, but my body said rest was necessary before I could engage in another one.

I had a three-week supply of sermons in my arsenal, more than enough, even if it should go longer than three weeks. But I knew in my heart the direction of my ministry was about to change.

This revival, however, would not be a solo event. It was reinforced by a mighty duo—my grandmother, aka Sister Scoma, and my aunt Elizabeth. With me, this trio had a strong presence.

I mentioned Grandma earlier regarding my phone conversation with Brother Mangrum because I assumed his call was for her to come to his church and preach, not me.

Grandma was a little over four feet with a heavy Italian accent, but she was mighty. Many churches invited her to share her testimony. The story she shared was of her conversion in her late twenties from Catholicism to Protestantism.

She served as a licensed minister in the Assemblies of God, and her zeal and love for God were contagious. A big part of Grandma's ministry was helping small churches rebuild. She would assist them by preaching until they acquired a pastor for their church.

Then there was my aunt Elizabeth, sister to my daddy and daughter to my grandma. Are you confused yet?

Liz and I were always close, almost like sisters. She was the youngest of her seven siblings, and I was the oldest of my eight siblings. To keep everyone confused, I was one year older than my aunt Liz. She was the talented musician of our group. My aunt played the piano, organ, and accordion. I no longer would have to play the accordion or sing solo. We would be singing together in each service.

Preaching would be my main contribution to our evangelist team. However exhausted I was after preaching, I continued to pray for the sick and with those who came to the altar for salvation.

Grandma, in her sweet but forceful Italian manner, shared her testimony in each service to the delight of the congregation. Everyone loved Sister Scoma, even if they couldn't understand her English pronunciation sometimes.

Our evangelistic team represented three generations. We became better known as the Scoma girls. Our unique ministry was launched after the Love Field revival.

The Love Field revival also continued for three weeks. I felt sure I was at the crossroads Brother Noah had told us about in his sermon on Senior Sunday. Other pastors were calling to schedule us to come to their churches.

How could I continue to work a full-time job at Sears and preach?

Preparing for a revival required more time for study and my necessary prayer time.

Something had to change.

My calling into the ministry was top priority.

So how should I handle this dilemma? I had taken the job at Sears as a favor to my daddy, who had arranged to get me hired when I was only sixteen.

It was an honor to have such a prestigious secretary job to an attorney. My own office space was located next to my boss's office.

However, my calling into ministry had changed everything.

I had to choose the calling of God or Sears. Disappointing Jesus or my daddy. I desperately needed clear direction from God.

It became clear I couldn't do both. I needed a plan to move forward.

As a Christian, I had learned whenever I had to make an important life decision, I should go on a fast. When I fasted and prayed, my spirit grew stronger and my selfish desires diminished. Then I could discern God's will for my life instead of my own.

This was an important life-changing decision.

I decided to fast until I had clarity about my situation, so I made a vow before God not to eat again until he assured me what to do and how to do it. I wasn't sure how long the fast would last, but I knew I would not eat food again until I heard his directions.

There is power in fasting. Isaiah 58:11 describes the purpose of fasting. God hears our voices when we fast. "And the LORD shall guide thee continually, and satisfy thy soul in drought, and make fat thy bones: and thou shalt be like a watered garden, and like a spring of water, whose waters fail not."

Desperate before God, I knew he would not forsake my desire to serve him. After all, he was the one who showed me how to use the sickle. Furthermore, He declared that together we would glean the field.

The first three days of the fast were difficult. I only drank water.

Because Adam ate the forbidden food, he lost his intimate relationship with God. Our intimate relationship with God was regained by Jesus when he ate no food for forty days. He was not in the comfort of a home as I was when I began my fast; he was in the desert.

Working eight hours a day at Sears and preaching every night at the revival was becoming a challenge. I wasn't sure how long the fast would last, but I was sure I would not eat again until I knew God's direction for me.

During my lunch hour at Sears, I sat at the table with my coworkers as they ate. The aroma of food didn't tempt me. I took advantage of the hour to drink my water and read over my sermon for that evening's service. Overwhelmed by my strength and energy, I believe God must have sent his angels to minister to me during this time. At the end of my forty days of fasting, I was stronger and more energized than when I first began. At the end of my forty-day fast, my mind was clear and the direction for my life was an absolute now.

I would go as soon as God cleared the way.

Let's Make a Deal with God

It was time to make another deal with God. My deal: If he wanted me to quit my job at Sears, then my boss would have to come to me. I wanted him to say I was no longer needed due to downsizing. Not fired. I even marked the spot where I wanted him to stand.

I was reminded about Gideon in the Bible. He was a farm boy from the country who had no formal training in leading armies. But he was faithful to his God. He wanted to be sure of his calling to fight the Midianites. He asked God if he would give him a sign so he could be sure. He put out a fleece before the Lord (Judges 6:40) to prove the Angel of the Lord's message was his true calling.

I too had no formal training, and I was being asked by God to go to battle as well. My fleece before the Lord involved how I was to be let go at Sears. On a piece of paper, I carefully pinned the words I wanted to hear from my boss. I also described the exact spot where I wanted him to stand as he spoke to me.

Like Gideon, it might appear I was doubting God, but my intentions were also desperate. The words I wrote were "I don't know how to say this, but since you are the youngest member of our team and we are cutting back on staff, I'm going to have to let you go." I wanted him to stand in front of my typewriter desk when he said this.

The following Monday morning, as I was getting settled in at my desk, it happened. Overlooking Dallas from my seventh-floor view, the sun was sneaking through the half-opened blinds and my opened window. My typewriter was on the desk behind me. I heard someone playing with the carriage, moving it back and forth. Who would be playing with my typewriter so early in the morning?

I whirled around in my swivel chair to see my boss standing there. He was pushing the carriage back and forth. By the look on his face, I observed something was wrong. I remained in my chair and moved closer to my typewriter. "Is there a problem?" I asked. The moments seemed eternal before he spoke.

He began, "I don't know how—"

I quickly interrupted him, "One moment, please." I reached into my desk drawer to retrieve my fleece, the paper on which I had written my agreement with God. Shyly, I said, "I am so sorry to interrupt you, but what were you saying?"

He continued pushing my typewriter carriage back and forth. He cleared his throat. "I don't know how to say this, but since you are the youngest member of our team, and we are cutting back on staff, I'm going to have to let you go."

I pushed my swivel chair back, jumped to my feet, and stood straight as though an army drill sergeant had called me to attention. After regaining my military-like composure, my voice came to attention as well. I quietly said, "Thank you, Jesus."

He said, "Excuse me? You're not upset with me?"

"Absolutely not," I replied. "You are an answer to my prayers."

My heart pounded from the excitement and relief from the unknown. I was still standing at "attention." In my excitement, the words "When would you like for me to leave?" leaped from my mouth.

He was still standing in amazement at my response. In his not-so-sure voice, he said, "Anytime."

Within ten minutes, my desk was spotless and cleared. As I was preparing to leave, he came back to my desk. This time with a big smile, he informed me that a nice severance package would be waiting for me in HR when I left.

Waiting for God's timing is always best but not the easiest. Abraham chose not to wait for God's blessing and promise. He missed God's best for him.

My severance package was more than I could ever imagine. It provided me the ability to buy an entire new wardrobe necessary for my new position as an evangelist. Now, I would be able to travel any distance to preach revivals.

Nothing was holding me back, or was there something?

I knew Grandma would be willing to go wherever we were asked. Liz was still in school, so how would we handle the situation? In God's time. I was sure he would arrange events to happen so we could travel together as a team.

CHAPTER 3

─────── ✐ ───────

An Unlikely Team

The Love Field church was located close to the airport. Sometimes, the sound of planes landing was riveting, but when their engines were at full power for takeoff, it became a challenge. It was an achievement to keep everyone's attention when the windows rattled and the roof swayed to the beat of the departing jets.

The transition from planes to the unusual team about to be introduced at the podium was no longer competition. All eyes and ears quickly focused on the three generations of Italian women being introduced. *Unusual* was an apt adjective to describe this grandmother, daughter, and granddaughter.

The advertised material read, "Teenage girl preaches each night, Grandmother shares her testimony, and Aunt Elizabeth plays the accordion and sings."

*****

One early spring Sunday after lunch, Grandma said she needed to talk to me.

Oh my, what had I done now?

After the dishes were cleared from the dining room table, Grandma and I sat down to talk. She wanted to tell me about an invitation she had recently received from James Leslie, the pastor in Linden, Texas. He had invited her to come preach at his church.

She looked directly into my eyes. "The Lord has impressed upon me that you are to preach this revival."

I frowned. "Where's Linden?"

"It's about a three-hour drive from here."

"Wow," I said. "But I can't even drive yet, and Elizabeth is only fifteen."

"I'll be your chauffeur," she said. "We could call ourselves 'the travelling evangelists.'"

I got excited. With my severance money in hand, I'd already shopped for my much-needed wardrobe, and I could afford to pay for the expenses to Linden.

Liz withdrew from high school so she could travel with me. We spent several days shopping for matching outfits. As the time grew near, we became so excited about this new venture that God had impressed upon my grandmother.

Linden, here comes the Scoma girls!

We never imagined this revival would last more than three weeks when we packed our bags and headed in Grandma's little green car for Linden, Texas.

What is a girl supposed to do? We packed enough clothes for a three-week revival, but it lasted for six weeks.

As the crowds expanded beyond belief, the revival went forward each night with robust enthusiasm. It looked as though everyone in Linden wanted to come and hear the young girl preach and the talented young musician.

The enthusiasm from Cass County was *beyond all thinking.* Several blocks away, the courthouse square installed loudspeakers to accommodate the overflow of attendees.

The crowds became so massive the church hired the local police and safety department to control the traffic. Pickup trucks came loaded with the beds full of family and friends and parked close by to hear the singing and sermon. There were no seats available inside, but the open windows allowed people to hear. It was Texas, and it was hot. The fans worked to the maximum to keep people as comfortable as possible.

Whenever we gave an altar call, those who were seated on the inside and wanted to accept Jesus as their Lord and Savior had to consider others outside. Those sitting at the courthouse or the churchyard or those in their trucks and cars were given extra time to make their way through the crowds. Ushers even escorted people from the courthouse through the traffic.

The pews of many of the other churches were empty, so the pastors decided to attend the revival and encouraged their congregation to do the same, worshipping with this unique team of women regardless of denomination.

The small town of Linden, Texas, had never witnessed such an event in any church before the "girls" arrived—a life-changing revival for many people, both young and old.

Waymon, a handsome young bachelor who worked at the Linden Post Office, came across one of the brochures left on the counter. Noting our picture on the brochure, he decided to come and check us out. And check us out he did.

Waymon was awestruck with what he saw and heard. Thinking his preacher brother, Brother Billy, might be interested in meeting the girls, he sent him a copy of the brochure. It just so happened Brother Billy was conducting a revival in Avery, Texas, thirty miles from Linden. A week earlier, Waymon had accepted Jesus as his Savior during this revival and was baptized by his brother.

The revival services in Avery ended, but the revival in Linden continued strong with no end in sight. Free for the next few weeks, Billy decided to come and support the revival in Linden. And perhaps there'd be an opportunity for the Jones boys to meet the Scoma girls.

We were delighted to meet the Jones boys. Billy was an asset to the Linden revival with his evangelistic zeal for God. The enthusiastic audience enjoyed Billy's testimony also. Grandma continued to share her testimony and her journey to becoming a Pentecostal preacher. Her story was always a joy for the audience.

Eventually, after an already-lengthy service, it came time for me to preach. The anxious but patient overflowing crowd certainly got their money's worth—three sermons each night.

The Linden revival began June 21, 1953, and ended in late July. The boys attended every night after Billy's schedule was free. The brothers were not sailors, like Liz and I had imagined we would marry when we were little girls playing grown-up house. But the brothers both became preachers.

As a bubbly teenage evangelist, my calling in ministry was very important to me, and I took it seriously. I was an exception to the rule when it came to romance. No dating while in revival.

We would hang around after church to visit, but usually, it was brief for me. Preaching and singing every night were exhausting. My entire being was focused on my preaching and praying with the people that came forward each night at the end of my sermons. The Jones brothers, however, were interested in more earthy endeavors— the Scoma girls—and they wanted to spend more time with us.

The local diner stayed open late and was our hangout after church. If we were to learn more about these boys, we had to make time after church. The diner, with its eight tables and one waitress, was our only option in this small town. Dating was not a prerogative for me or Liz.

Early every morning, on his way to work in his brand-new 1953 Mercury, Waymon drove by the house where we were staying. With a special apparatus on his fancy muffler, he'd announce his presence with a wham bang, loud enough to wake up the dead or my neighbors.

I hurried to the window and waved as he drove slowly past our house. The funny feelings I was having perplexed me. I began to think maybe I liked him, entranced by his subtle attention to me. Still, I had to stay focused on the revival.

My days found me secluded in prayer and studying for the evening service. The evenings of preaching, singing, and praying for the needs of people left me exhausted. I had no desire for entertaining anyone. Rest and preparation for the next evening were paramount.

After six spectacular weeks, the Linden revival ended. Other revivals were waiting for us to begin shortly, but the break was just enough time for the boys to capture our hearts.

Billy decided Lizzy was his missing link. He needed her musical talent for his ministry to be complete.

Waymon felt he could be a great asset to my ministry. After all, he drove a new Mercury, and I would need another chauffeur soon. I must not forget he taught me how to drive it.

It looked like Grandma would be traveling solo again. As events began to materialize, it appeared Liz and I would be ministering in different paths. How would I deal with this? I'd have to play and sing solo again.

And we would no longer be known as the Scoma girls.

Beyond All Thinking: Despite Circumstances

Abnormal: unusual, rare, uncommon, uncharacteristic, deviating from the usual or norm.

This describes my precourtship days.

Unusual: In high school most girls have dated. *Rare:* I was not allowed to date alone, only with church groups. *Uncharacteristic:* Daddy ruled.

For Daddy's own reasons, no one was qualified to date me. His job as a good dad, he assumed, was to protect and guard his "little" girl. Time had moved forward, and I was a big girl now. In just a few months, I would be eighteen. But Daddy's rules of no alone dating were still enforced.

This was a real dilemma. I met an eligible guy, and we liked each other. What would Daddy's reactions be when I introduced the two of them? I became anxious. I didn't want to become so involved that one or both of us would be hurt if Daddy said no.

As soon as there were a few days free in my schedule, Waymon and I drove to Dallas to meet with my parents. I was uneasy. What would my daddy say to him? What kind of questions would he ask? After all, I didn't have all the answers about him either. I'd only spent a month with Waymon.

It turned out I didn't need to worry. Waymon did a great job interacting with my parents. Momma as usual had prepared her famous, tantalizing meatloaf, with her garlic mashed potatoes and green beans. This certainly set the stage for the much-anticipated get-acquainted time with Waymon and my family. Momma lowered the tension level when she came dashing out of the kitchen with her mouthwatering chocolate meringue pie.

Everyone, including my youngest four siblings, seemed to be on their best behavior, for which I was grateful. Even baby Camille.

My parents were impressed with the guy. So much so that my daddy gave us his blessings and accepted him immediately. Why?

1. He worked for the post office, so he could provide for me.
2. He was ten years my senior and mature and could take care of me.
3. He was a veteran.
4. He was a Christian, the most important of all.

After Daddy's scrutiny, Waymon qualified. Daddy's fatherly advice to us was "the rest is up to you." Momma thought he was polite, and my siblings also accepted him with open arms because he played games with them.

The windshield wipers, working at a steady rhythm, forced me to focus on my struggles at this moment. The return trip to Linden was much different. My mind was going in a myriad of directions. The drops of rain hitting our windshield were comforting. God would also be in control of this interruption in my ministry.

Ministry, my most important focus, was now being tested. Another person was about to enter my already-committed life.

More revivals were waiting to be conducted. Could I remain focused? The thought of planning an Italian wedding would be a challenge.

Waymon was twenty-eight years old and a bachelor. A war veteran, and now, I, a young girl of eighteen, was about to become his fiancée. I was still shaken by this unexpected interruption of my ministry.

A week later after our return from Dallas, Waymon asked for a date night. Excited to finally get to learn more about him, I said yes. There had been few opportunities for us to spend any alone time together. I wasn't sure where we were going, but I knew it was going to be special by the excitement in his voice.

His new Mercury was spiffy when he pulled up that night at my house. It had been freshly waxed and shined from the front hood to the rear bumper. When I anxiously answered the door, he looked so handsome. My adrenaline was flowing at the sound of his voice.

During the drive, our words were few, and the silence was piercing. What was on his mind? I was on unfamiliar, dimly lit roads. My nerves were on edge, especially when I noticed his brow was wet from perspiration. At the next junction, I had every reason to become nervous. The road where we turned pointed to the cemetery.

Cemetery?

Why was he taking me to the cemetery?

Was the pressure too much of a life change for him? Was there a possibility the man my parents thought was so amazing could be a murderer? I would soon find out.

As soon he found a spot to park the car near a clump of trees overlooking the city, he climbed out of the car. Calmly, he walked around to my door, opened it, and asked if I would step out. In a low but steady voice, he said, "I have something to show you."

A gun or a knife? I wondered.

Waymon reached for my shaking hand and led me to a bench close by. I was composed by now, and he asked me to sit down after he had wiped off the damp seat.

He positioned himself in front of me and knelt on one knee.

I was so relieved when I finally understood his intentions.

I felt the tears that I was trying to control dampen my anxious face.

In his deep, steady voice, he held my hand between his and asked, "Will you marry me?"

My elated reply came with the continual flow of tears.

"Yes, I will marry you."

He took my clammy left hand and placed an engagement ring on my finger.

Both memorable and different, my engagement cannot be forgotten.

How many women are proposed to in a cemetery? I'm still wondering why he chose such a site. Did he think it was romantic? I never asked.

Liz and I usually did everything together, and our engagements were no different. Billy also took her to the cemetery for her engagement encounter. Did the boys plan this? And why?

Once again, I was facing a crossroad of challenges, but God's calling remained top priority in my life. Could I manage a ministry and a marriage and let neither fail?

Since Liz and I always made most major life decisions together. Meeting our guys and getting engaged were not any different. Billy needed a companion for his ministry, and Liz was certainly the talented woman he needed.

Our wedding days were two weeks apart. The Scoma girls would soon become the Jones girls.

The time had come to divide the ministry and hopefully conquer. It appeared the Scoma girls and Grandma would soon have new roles in ministry. Liz and I would soon be walking down our different church aisles to become the Jones girls.

What were we going to do with Grandma?

The Scoma evangelistic team would no longer be a team. Billy was taking Grandma's baby girl for his bride and ministry companion. Waymon and I would be building our ministry together as a husband and wife team.

The primary goal for each of us gals was to establish our respective ministries with a greater harvest of souls. Regardless of where our travels would take us, we would be two teams now, plus Grandma. While churches waited for their new pastors, she would continue sharing her testimony whenever and wherever asked.

CHAPTER 4

―― ⚬ ――

Let the New Journey Begin

My wedding day would be a beautiful traditional Italian wedding. Beyond reasonable thinking, all my little-girl dreams were coming true. Sixty days after our engagement announcement, we would be married.

How would clinical pastoral counselors address such a situation today? Impossible and not recommended.

In my practice today, premarital counseling requires a minimum of six months of sessions after an engagement is announced, but counseling was not required in the early fifties or widely practiced.

Sixty days after our engagement announcement, it was our wedding day, October 1, 1953. We were confident. We didn't need counseling, nor did we need a wedding planner even with a guest list of three hundred requiring RSVPs.

A custom-designed wedding gown in sixty days? That would take a miracle.

Custom designed wedding gown

The wedding gown of my dreams caused Ms. Vi, my designer, some sleepless nights. She and I visited a bridal shop to see the gown I wanted. On her knees, Ms. Vi examined the dress and took notes. She decided she could make my dream wedding gown. To my surprise, she announced it was to be her gift to me.

The cathedral train was not an ordinary one; it was more than I could have imagined. I had dreamed of a spectacular train flowing behind me, but Ms. Vi's talented hands wove pearls and rhinestones into the full-length train. Numerous fittings followed, but in thirty days, a bride's dream came true.

In addition to her amazing workload, there were my seven bridesmaids and a maid and matron of honor to dress. Ms. Vi also designed and completed them in another twenty-five days. A total of twenty-seven friends and family made up our wedding party.

Certainly not to be forgotten for this marathon wedding was the reception. This included locating the venue, food, and entertainment. My parents made certain everything would be memorable.

My pastor, H. C. Noah, performed the beautiful ceremony. He had been part of my life since I was a young child and involved in my calling to the ministry.

Arches surrounded the sanctuary and white picket fences that were covered with a vast array of pink and white flowers. Violins and the Hammond organ filled the sanctuary with the selected music that accompanied the twenty-seven-member choir.

The choir sang the verses of "Here Comes the Bride," and a proud daddy anxiously walked his firstborn down the winding aisle covered in pink rose petals. My brother, Lou, was chosen as best man to walk with the groom.

Our ceremony concluded with both of us receiving Holy Communion. This was our sealed covenant before God.

After the wedding frenzy and lavish Italian reception we left for our honeymoon in Galveston, Texas. I had looked forward to this time to organize my new life and learn more about my new husband. The role of wife would add new responsibilities for me as an evangelist. But we enjoyed our honeymoon exploring the island and each other.

Evangelizing Continues

Waymon, a new Christian and new to ministry, was supportive of me and my role as an evangelist. We would resume my already-scheduled revivals as a couple. This was going to require a tremendous amount of travel.

Since Liz was no longer with me, I had to sing solo again, in addition to playing the accordion and organ on occasion and preaching. Evangelizing kept us on the move. We conducted revivals from Texas to Oklahoma, Louisiana, Kentucky, Arkansas, New Mexico, and Michigan.

Waymon was an enormous behind-the-scene help for me. He took responsibility for all the household chores and cooking our meals while I studied and prepared for each service.

Shortly after I realized I was pregnant with our first child, our travel conditions changed. We purchased a mobile home. This was our home away from home.

Noticeably pregnant, I required more rest.

As Waymon began to grow from a young Christian, he too felt God's calling on his life to minister. He began to testify a little more in each service about God's grace. We were eager to see how God would lead us into a dual ministry.

The time had come.

In Dallas, Texas, in the same hospital where I was born, our baby girl was born May 7, 1955. We named her Deborah Louann. She was the darling of every church, regardless of where we might be ministering. There were never a lack of babysitters or people to spoil her. The abundance of candy and bubble gum also caused frequent visits to the dentist office.

A significant issue as a new mom and preacher was breastfeeding my baby.

Arranging Deborah's schedule to work with mine for earlier feedings was not always successful. Sometimes it was a challenge to nurse her, then hurry back to the stage. Most times she was content, and if nursing didn't work, there was an emergency bottle. The audiences were so kind and understanding. If necessary, they would sing another song or two until I finished my motherly duty.

Our intense travelling days could be overwhelming at times with a small child, and we just learned our second child was on the way. We were scheduled for only one revival in Cadillac, Michigan, and the 1,543-mile journey was sure to be a challenge. With our trailer in tow, from Albuquerque, New Mexico to Cadillac, Michigan, we remained in Michigan for another six months.

When our final revival in Michigan ended, we'd be heading back to Texas for our son to be born. It was a difficult decision for us to leave the wonderful people in Michigan, even though I was pregnant. Waymon was doing a great job with our daughter and additional duties that I could not complete with my study and prayer time.

The Michiganders were wanting us to stay in Michigan, and our son could be born there. They loved my Southern accent, singing, and preaching. They had never experienced a young girl preacher like me before. But a young girl? I was twenty-one and didn't think of myself as a young girl. A young mother—yes.

They kept us busy all the time we were there. I preached and sang every night for those six months. My schedule included preaching at the revival church and a conference or youth rally nearby. Yet my body was talking to me. I would need to take a break and soon.

It was becoming more difficult to sing and play the accordion over my baby bump. I notified the remaining scheduled pastors concerning my pregnancy. I was sure they would want to cancel their revival.

None cancelled.

Nothing seemed to stop the crowds from coming to church, not even the night that eight feet of new snow fell. I was sure no one would want to venture out into such conditions. I even suggested to the pastor to cancel the service.

His reply to me, "Are you kidding?"

Forgive me, Lord, for thinking eight feet of snow could keep those Christians home. We would always remember the people of Michigan for their zeal and love for God and his Word.

Another amazing memory of Michigan occurred in Reed City with a visit to the home of George Bennard, composer of "The Old Rugged Cross." On a hill not far from his home stood a modest wooden cross as a memorial. He and his wife, Hannah, were such gracious hosts to sign a copy of the song as well as show us his original handwritten copy.

The Reverend George Bennard died October 10, 1958, at the age of eighty-five shortly after our visit in 1957.

We were desperate now to return to Texas before our son was born. Time was critical if he was to be born a Texan. Timing was everything.

We made it.

In just two months on April 26, 1957, our baby boy, Daniel Waymon, was also born in Dallas, Texas, at the same hospital as his sister and mother.

In a few short years of our ministry together, Waymon's calling as a minister was leading him into a pastoral role of leadership. He began his studies to prepare for his calling as pastor. Later, accepted at Asbury Theological Seminary to continue his studies, he earned his master of divinity. His ministry as teacher/preacher and mine as evangelist were a great combination for our congregations.

On November 2, 1958, I was ordained by Thomas Zimmerman, who later became the longest-serving general superintendent of twenty-six years with the Assemblies of God. We were new pastors in the Arkansas District when I was ordained—the youngest woman in the Assemblies of God denomination to be ordained. I was twenty-three.

As different as our ministries were, God put the package together for us to become pastors and equipped us to build churches. Waymon's ministry leaned toward teaching and leadership, and mine evangelism and motivational speaking.

With a four- and two-year-old now, traveling became more of a challenge. When we received an invitation from Bradley, Arkansas, we were excited. We welcomed their invitation to become the pastors of their church. This was going to be a big change for our ministry, but we accepted the challenge. Along with this opportunity, we soon learned that baby number 3 was on the way.

Our little family continued to grow. However, our little girl would not be born a Texan but an Arkie. Deanna Ruth was born September 28, 1959, in Lewisville, Arkansas.

We thought our little family was complete. Doctors had told us that after a surgical procedure to remove an ovary with a growth the size of a grapefruit, we should not expect other pregnancies. That was the doctor's diagnosis. Four years later, it was overruled from above. What a surprise and blessing when we learned baby number 4 would soon join her three siblings.

This little blessing was such a bundle of joy. Darla Sue was born September 25, 1963, in Atlanta, Texas.

Pastoral duties and being a mother of four active children seemed overwhelming at times. I too had to prepare sermons, in addition to playing the organ/piano for each service. But motherhood was my favorite job. While the exhausting responsibilities seemed unbearable sometimes, the endless love we shared as a family made it worthwhile.

My first priority was our children, then the home, and then the church family. Our first assignment from God was to be parents to our four little ones. The church, its staff, and the members weren't accountable to God for our children. We were. If we won multitudes to Christ and lost our own children, we would have lost everything.

It's amazing how many roles the pastor is expected to be responsible for with the congregation. Some members expect his involvement in every activity. Preparing and delivering sermons was only the beginning of the pastor's week. Working with others to repair or build the church was also expected from him. The housebound, hospitalized, and those with spiritual issues also needed house calls or hospital visits.

At twenty-eight, I was overwhelmed by the demanding projects expected of me, the pastor's wife. The responsibilities of a wife, mother, and pastor's wife and preacher became an intense balancing act.

While we travelled as evangelists, we were not attached to an individual church. Our home and ministry were attached behind our car—we were always on the move. Our new role had us attached to a church and its congregation. Now I realized how immune we were from the many pastoral duties when we traveled.

We thought it was our responsibility to meet all the church's expectations of us. Pastoring was a role neither of us were prepared for. New sets of problems constantly appeared, all needing resolution.

We were introduced to our first church as pastors, while they were engaged in remodeling their sanctuary. It was later discovered the building had severe structural issues before the project could be completed. This added to everyone's stress. The committees, board members, and congregation seemed to have different points of view on how things should be handled. We soon realized we could only please some of the people some of the time but not all the people all the time. So we did what we thought was best for the entire congregation.

Pastors of smaller congregations were expected to do more physical work and become engaged in more activities than churches with larger staffs. An additional need was to work outside the church since the weekly offering varied from month to month. It was quite common for pastors to have to supplement their income just to afford the necessities.

It was only a matter of time until the stress took its toll on us, both emotionally and physically, just as it had on other pastors before us who were more experienced. Their stories were painful as well. They shared with us how they too felt alone and unappreciated for their many sacrifices. Their health and marriages were also being affected.

Some pastors' wives I was acquainted with were as lonely as I was. Outside of our immediate church duties, there was little pastoral fellowship.

Who was available that could be trusted to be confided in? Our responsibilities as home builders and wives for our very busy husbands left us lonely. Our husbands were too busy with ministerial responsibilities.

Often promises for family time and date nights were broken. There didn't seem to be a solution to our dilemma. We were victims, lost in the hustle-bustle of God's work. My needs were no different from those of many other pastors' wives. We tried to wear a smile and stay involved as much as possible. If we were able to maintain the façade, people would assume everything was okay. But my life was going awry. I felt I was dying inside as a woman, and nobody really cared about my needs or feelings.

Whenever a pastor had to work another job or spend endless hours at the church, he was unavailable for his family. The growing needs of the children required a surrogate to intercede. Most often, that surrogate was the mom.

In my circumstances, at times I had to be both mom and dad to our children. More stress for me and less time for me and my husband. The walls of unity were starting to crumble right in front of me. The togetherness no longer existed. We were a divided house.

Solitude had become my best friend. Even though I was surrounded by a community of Christians, they were unaware of the hidden pain I could not talk about.

As Christian leaders, could this be happening in our home? We were both so busy doing God's work, and yet we were falling apart on the inside. That couldn't have been God's plan for us. Being busy all the time wasn't what God had in mind when he asked us to *feed his sheep*. Nor was it his plan for the ministry to supersede raising a family.

My husband, a good man, was the best dad possible for his young family. But while he was subsidizing our income, it was necessary for me to become both mom and dad for most of the school activities for our children.

Eventually, I began to see cracks appearing in our already-weakened marital foundation. Exhausted, I searched my heart and asked myself, what more could I have done to help my husband? Already the copastor, organist, women's leader, coordinator of special events, and the mother of our four children. What was I missing?

Alone time.

We needed time for just the two of us.

Time to communicate our feelings regarding each other's needs.

Rejection and abandonment had begun to leave me feeling distanced from my husband. I needed and wanted his comforting hand and words and to feel cherished by him.

As a couple, there must be something we could do to change our drifting apart. What concerns were most important to my husband? Could we make each other a priority, or was it too late?

Time was not a friend of mine. I waited each day for Waymon to notice how lonely I was. When nothing changed, it became clear that he didn't seem to care, so I suppressed my feelings and kept myself busy. I threw myself into my children's school activities.

Yet I felt communication was important, so I reminded my husband how much time I had to spend with our children because he was always too busy to meet his family's needs.

He always responded with a shrug. "I can't do it all," or "Your attitude's just making things worse."

My daily prayer was to be the best mom I could for our four Ds. I continued to stay involved with their immediate needs both at home and school. Our number one goal for our four children was for them to love God and to serve him with all their hearts. We wanted them to live normal lives and not just be preacher's kids (PKs). They went to ball games and played baseball. They went to the bowling alley with their friends. My girls wore jeans to school, the disapproval of some "church folks" notwithstanding.

A few parishioners and deacons questioned my parenting skills. On many occasions, I reminded them that God had given me that responsibility, and they had no worries. I would suggest everyone to take a deep breath and enjoy the PKs.

I decided as their pastor's wife I was going to remain being the best mom possible as a role model for others. Arguments from finances to control issues seemed to prevail at the church. It was taking a toll on Waymon. He did not enjoy confrontations and, as a private individual, would not express his feelings or thoughts.

Perhaps our marriage could have become healthy again if my husband's responsibilities were less stressful, but conflict never seemed to lighten. Despite my yearning for my husband's love and attention, I realized Waymon had been chosen by God to be the head of our family and the church. It was my responsibility to respect and to honor him.

What changes could I make to get my husband back? How could I get him to focus on our private life? Our communication skills were almost nonexistent. My past efforts were not working. Perhaps I could try a little harder and show more affection and appreciation?

Affection? Appreciation? Would he have time to even notice?

Why was I good at most everything else in life but I was a failure at being Waymon's wife?

While we struggled as young ministers to do our Father's will, I thought of Joseph and his coat of many colors that represented his father's favor. How his jealous brothers stripped it from him before his destiny was fulfilled. Joseph had to endure trial after trial after his brothers sold him into slavery before gaining favor with Egypt's pharaoh.

I often identified with Joseph when the denomination we faithfully served did not have programs in place to help struggling young ministers and their families. Joseph was alone and separated from those he loved while in the Egyptian prison. We were in prison of our own ministry.

Intensity of aloneness was like a rumbling volcano ready to erupt. Slowly damaging the foundation of our marriage. The foundation was cracking. What was our plan of escape when it erupted?

Continuing to wear my many hats, I desperately wanted our family to be healthy. We managed a good front for the next twelve years. God was faithful; we survived many disappointments during those years as we continued to pastor.

CHAPTER 5

———— ✑ ————

1953–1979: From Bliss to This

We continued pastoring churches from Oklahoma to Arkansas, Texas, Louisiana, and finally to Kentucky. Our children, no longer babies, were in middle and high school.

Our marriage was not as it appeared; we were in survival mode. All our efforts focused on trying to keep our ministry functioning.

Job burnout eventually led to the slow death of our marriage, along with physical and emotional exhaustion. Without professional counseling, all signs led to an imminent death of our twenty-five-year marriage.

We needed professional Christian counseling if our marriage was to survive. Both of us would have to agree to seek help. It's sad but true many times only one spouse recognizes the need for counseling, and they're not the problem. Often this one-sidedness results in divorce.

We both needed help.

My husband had hurt me deeply, but I didn't trust anyone enough to confide in regarding the situation. I was living with rejection from the man I had promised to love "until death do us part." I kept the pain well hidden. But I couldn't conceal the resentment that was always there. I swept my hurts under the rug, but they manifested themselves at the most inconvenient times, usually when we least expect it.

I believed my husband liked me but did not love me. His behavior had changed toward me over the years. Now he was more like a judge than a loving husband. I responded to him as "not guilty, your honor." Humiliation, disappointment, and anger combined inside me; and I lost all hope for our marriage.

What expectations still remained after twenty-five years of marriage? What changes could we make that could give us hope to continue with the next twenty-five?

There is a term I use in my clinical Christian counseling practice to describe why divorce is nothing more than a Band-Aid on an open wound. The Band-Aid doesn't heal the wound; it only covers the infection. Still the infection remains and needs more than a Band-Aid.

It's a painful process while the infection is being removed for healing to begin. Like most, we also preferred to avoid the pain, hoping it would eventually go away on its own. I describe this as "scooping the goop." It is necessary to remove the goop in order to get to the core that's causing the infection. Once the core of the infection is reached, restoration and healing can begin.

If the real issues of a marriage needing restoration are not addressed, they will result in an infected life. Usually, it goes from a series of disappointments to a life of resentment. If the problems are only covered with a Band-Aid, the infectious core remains—it gets worse.

My husband, ten years my senior, served in the armed forces, received a college education, and lived on his own while I was growing up. I had not experienced life outside my home and church and had no experience with relationships with the opposite sex. I was my husband's virgin bride.

A passive person, Waymon didn't like to make decisions if he thought it would involve conflict. This was evident in reprimanding our children or handling conflict in the church. He did very little of either in both cases if he thought he would not be liked or respected.

We hadn't set boundaries as a couple. Considering we only knew each other for thirty days before our short sixty-day wedding, many of our conflicts grew into stalemates. Most ended in disappointing decisions.

It was obvious how we shared roles as pastors. I overstepped our unestablished boundaries many times. Frustrated, I would make decisions whenever he wasn't sure what to do or avoided doing anything.

There was always plenty of conversation between us but limited communication. If I wanted to discuss marriage issues, he avoided discussing anything negative. He was confident if I changed, all our issues would be resolved. His self-denial only worsened our situation.

Expressing feelings was much easier for me than it was for my husband. He was cautious in his thinking and reserved whenever he spoke. It was difficult for him to commit to anything unless he was certain there would be no misunderstanding. Conversation was less of a challenge than to communicate. To communicate would involve being vulnerable. However, he could give a great sermon.

As a temperament therapist, I now clearly understand the conflict that raged in his life and our lives as a couple. Waymon preferred peace at any cost, and he avoided anything that would interfere with it. His thinking was if you don't talk about it, it will go away, even if you must sweep it under the bedroom rug.

The Other Side of the Bedroom Door

Come with me as I allow you to peek around the other side of our bedroom door. We were two good people, parents of four beautiful children, pastors of a busy church, and engaged in another building program.

Our temperaments and behaviors clashed. There was neither interest nor time for us to talk about anything personal.

Results?

Many needs of mine not important or met.

My husband avoided discussions about personal needs. He did not like conflict.

Unkind behavior eventually became a method of control known and seen only by me.

It seemed that neither of us chose to work on restoring our broken marriage. I believed the marriage could be mended.

God was an expert at mending broken people. When God mends broken people, they become brand-new. He could even bring death back to living again.

In all my brokenness, sadness, and humiliation, I didn't know where to go or whom I could trust for help.

As an ordained minister, I should have the answers, right? What would other ministers think if they knew about our problems?

Like most of our minister friends, we all gave our best efforts to meet the needs of our congregation. They were priority.

It was considered a professional risk to have genuine friends to confide in within the church—ours or others.

Most ministers seemed to be in competition with each other and not supportive as a brotherhood. This affected both of us physically, emotionally, and spiritually. We needed the unconditional fellowship of other ministers. This was a missing link from our lives. A phone call or shared coffee time would have been a blessing.

Our marriage would soon die unless we did something to seek treatment to heal the infectious core. When we discussed our marital condition, Waymon seemed to think the only solution was divorce. When asked if that was what he wanted, his answer was, "I can handle a divorce."

Our marriage desperately needed to be cared for before it died. Once the root of a tree is dead, no matter how much you feed or water it, it's dead.

Likewise, our marriage was close to death. Only a miracle could save it. Of course, Jesus is known to bring life back to dead people. Jesus, the resurrection, was our only hope.

We continued to live in Danville, Kentucky, in the same home where years earlier we had begun a new Assemblies of God church and a child day care center in our basement. Within a year of meeting in our home, we were able to purchase a church building for our sanctuary.

After establishing an active congregation, we later resigned as pastors. Since we were no longer pastors, my husband accepted the position as principal of a Christian school in Louisville. He also lived in Louisville during the school week and drove the two-hour drive home each weekend. The possibility of divorce was often the focus of our conversations.

Those were stressful and anxious days for us. Most weekends resulted in a severe case of stomach cramps for me. I struggled hard to create a loving environment when he was home. I made his favorite foods, wore my nicest outfits, and managed to keep a smile on my face.

When I heard the engine of his Studebaker rev up, I knew I was off duty. He was heading back to his life in Louisville. No more pretense of the image my husband wanted people to see. He returned to being principal, and I returned to caring for my thirty-five students in the day care center in our basement.

Despite the many unsuccessful efforts to make our marriage work, it was obvious the roots of our marriage were dead. We were cordial most times, and we worked hard at liking each other. This was not the way our "forever after" was supposed to be, especially since we didn't believe in divorce.

After I finally realized my life was like a game of cards, I must play the cards that were dealt me. Sadly, the time came when I had to face reality; the last hand had been dealt. I lost the game of our struggling marriage.

Many hours of conversation followed concerning the faults of each other. We both finally agreed divorce was our *only* option. This was the hardest decision I ever had to make and the saddest.

Why did we lose something so precious?

We weathered the storm to make it to our twenty-fifth wedding anniversary.

There were hopes from family and friends that things could be different. We celebrated with a lovely party at our home hosted by our children and friends.

However, what should have been a happy celebration seemed to be just another day for my husband. Nothing had changed.

As was his normal behavior, he did nothing to acknowledge this special occasion. There were no flowers, cards, or gifts. Our children made reservations for the two of us at a nice restaurant.

The meal was lovely, but conversation was minimal.

The waiter brought our bill and laid it on our table. Without missing a beat, Waymon handed me the bill and said, "You'll have to pay. I don't have any money with me." It was obvious. The evening and occasion were not important.

The struggle to maintain the facade continued. Disappointments and loneliness continued with our separation.

Our struggling marriage continued to suffer with intense arguments.

Waymon finally agreed to counseling. But only one session.

The church office was in another city, a short drive from us.

After we were seated and greeted by the pastor/counselor, my husband immediately assured the counselor I was the one with the problem and needed the counseling. He also reminded the counselor he had no issues and would appreciate any help the pastor could give me.

This familiar remark reminded of a "Jesus" complex—he could do no wrong. However, I admitted my faults to the pastor and told him I did need his help. In fact, I was desperate to know what and how to change in order to save our marriage.

One session, however, would not be sufficient to solve all our conflicts.

Change is a difficult thing for everyone.

Much like a flat tire, it must be changed before you can go anywhere.

I was hurting, disappointed, and embarrassed and wanted to learn how to resolve our relationship issues so we could try to move forward with a better relationship. Our problems were no longer hidden in a corner. Family, friends, and church members noticed. If we chose to avoid professional help, we could no longer avoid a divorce.

Change meant both of us had to do something different in our marriage. And we couldn't change the other person, only ourselves. If we continued to go in the same destructive direction, we could expect destructive results. I didn't want a divorce at forty-three, and I don't think he wanted one either, but that was what would happen if there was no change in our direction.

No Winners in a Divorce

The word *divorce* represents division.

Division is always a painful process.

In any divorce, it is not only the tangible division of property but also the division of family and friends. Divorce also divides all the dreams of growing old together.

Divorce affects the lives of family members, both young and old. Some will be affected early and some later, but there is always a huge price to pay. There are always consequences to any divorce.

There are no good divorces.

Unless one has lived behind closed doors with the victims, we must keep guarded lips. There is always another story on the other side of the door. His and hers.

Compassionate Christian counseling for ministers was not available for us. However, help is available today with Christian counseling for ministers and their families in crisis called Emerge located in Akron, Ohio, and sponsored by the Assemblies of God. This service offers healthy pastors' seminars, marriage tune-ups, and marriage retreats in various locations, as well as mental and emotional help.

Spiritual and mental pressures remain a common thread among ministers and their spouses—maybe even more so. The need for a safe place for pastors and their families to express emotions and conflicts is important, of course, always in confidentiality.

How do I know?

I know because today as a pastoral Christian clinical counselor, I have helped to restore marriages and shattered homes. Pastors' children have gone astray because of the overwhelming cost of the ministers' priorities. Boundaries have been neglected with little focus on quality family time. The responsibilities of the church have taken priority, and the importance of the family has been devalued and neglected.

Emerge has ministered to more than 250,000 people, too late for us but an oasis for many broken lives today.

It was a difficult day for me when the door of our almost-twenty-six-year marriage closed for the final sting with the signing of divorce papers. Facing the consequences of a failed marriage was humbling.

Especially sad were the betrayals. Stranded by our denomination, who did not inquire or help with the struggles for us as young pastors. Without further inquiry, my pastoral license was revoked. I had served as an ordained minister for decades when the elected leadership I had served for decades considered me as an outcast minister.

How sad and disappointing without reaching out for both sides of the full story.

My husband, however, maintained his status as an ordained minister. It was determined that he had not filed for the divorce, even though he too had wanted the divorce. Even though we'd used the same attorney, this appeared to be a double standard.

My consolation: God knew the truth about our entire struggle from the beginning to the bitter end. I determined in my heart that I would emerge through the fire without the smell of smoke and still be gracious to him. He would always be the father of our four "Ds."

It's Not Who's Right or Wrong—Who Decides?

I needed restoration.

To continue the calling of God in ministry was most important. I never lost sight of God's special call in my life. He still loved me, and my life would be vibrant again. I didn't know when or how, but it would happen.

Our marriage was never a mistake; it was God ordained and sealed with our wedding covenant. But a lack of wisdom in how we handled difficulties was obvious. Our marriage was a beautiful entity; it produced four amazing, strong children who love and serve God, and each has their own families. So many life lessons along my journey have made it possible for me to continue to help others through Christian counseling to deal with these same issues.

My dreams as a teenager were to get married, have a family, and live happily ever after. I heard about divorces, but I never thought I would be among the statistics. But it happened. I became a statistic. I am a divorced woman. Divorced from my ministry and my amazing calling—the one since I was sixteen.

Where could a divorced female minister go from this juncture?

What I did in the past always helped. When not sure what to do, I would pray and wait for God's direction. Even in my aloneness, I knew God had not stopped loving me despite a failed marriage.

The lemon of divorce was bitter and difficult to squeeze at times, but squeeze it I did. I had to squeeze with all my might to make lemonade. Struggling to keep my family, home, and business intact required many sobering decisions from a forty-four-year-old single mom.

The day care center continued to operate at capacity with its thirty-five students and a two-year waiting list. Some parents registered their unborn children and even their anticipated pregnancies. Kiddie Land Day Care Center was widely known in Frankfort, Kentucky, the capital, for our devoted care of babies and children and our discipline.

My daughters were a tremendous help working in the center after school and during their summers off from college. Kiddie Land Day Care became a busy and happy place for me and a place of purpose for all of us.

Divorce should never become the concern of the children involved. Children are precious jewels from God. Since we are parents, being cordial to each other, before and after divorce, is the least that one can do to help them cope with the loss of a parent from the home.

Bitterness makes a bad situation worse for everyone. Negative words regarding the other parent can become engraved in the children's hearts and minds for a lifetime—even into their own marriages. Children should never know the private details that happen behind closed doors.

Lessons Learned

I learned many lessons in this chapter of my life.

1. Before a wedding date was set, my fiancé and I needed marriage counseling—the basics, what is marriage? The short time of knowing each other wasn't long enough. I only knew about marriage from observing my parents' marriage. Most moms and dads don't share their relationship in detail with their children.
2. The roles of evangelist, pastor's wife, and mother were more than I could handle sometimes. My mother was mother of eight children, but I wore too many different hats and needed someone to help me know how to cope.
3. Though a seemingly bleak future loomed ahead, I was able to move beyond my own thinking. My early life as part of a strong Christian family and the beautiful encounter with Jesus became my foundation. The many miracles, both physical and spiritual, in my ministry provided another layer. Even the disappointment and heartache built onto that foundation. There was purpose for all the hurt and life lessons that I needed to go through.
4. There is a tendency to become bitter and want to blame others when they betray us or keep us from accomplishing our dreams. It's not only embarrassing but sad that we must start all over to move forward again.

It's your turn.

1. What lessons did you learn from this chapter?
2. What lessons have you learned from marriage and divorce?

CHAPTER 6

—— ⌘ ——

1980: Life on the Move

I t was an ordinary, balmy evening at the running track in Danville, Kentucky. A normal day, but I didn't know my life was about to change.

The Centre College training track was one of my favorite places to train. My best friend, Marilyn, and her two children from my day care, Holly and Lance, were with me each evening, encouraging me as I completed each lap, preparing for another race. They would even run alongside me from time to time.

How could I have known this night I would meet my knight? And of all places, a college running track? When my knight finally caught up to me, his breathing was a little distressed as he struggled to tell me about his moment of awe.

"Before I got out of my car," he said, "while I was lacing my shoes, I looked up, and lo and behold, I saw you running, and I immediately fell in love."

A great pickup line. Right?

The man had a great sense of humor. He was an excellent conversationalist as well.

It was obvious he too worked out; however, I wasn't sure how serious he was about running. He was well put together in his running shorts. I noticed his legs as he approached the track with his towel thrown over his shoulder. Those legs were something to write home about.

It wasn't long before we were running side by side. He had me laughing. I couldn't remember when I'd last laughed so much. This guy must have been sent from God, I thought. Maybe God was sending me hope for a brighter future.

During one of my many laps around the track, my little buddies, Holly and Lance, eight and ten years old, would run alongside me for company. Marilyn, their mother, wasn't a runner but would bring along a novel to read while I was training for my marathon.

This charismatic man chose to run with the children after they dropped back from running beside me. Later, I found out it was an information-gathering run for him.

During the next lap around, one of them ran back to me. "Teacher Jones, he wants to know if you're married."

"No, there is no Mr. Jones."

In unison, they yelled, "She doesn't have a husband anymore."

That marked the end of the information-gathering run. Soon, he was running beside me again.

This knight certainly knew how to win a woman's heart. A warning sign flicked on. My pace picked up as did the adrenaline rush. My breathing was becoming shallow. What was it about this man without a name that made me want to turn and run away from him? My fight-or-flight hormone had kicked in.

Still reeling from the shock of my twenty-six-year failed marriage, I was a divorced woman and a minister, not ready to trust another man anytime soon. But it felt incredibly refreshing to laugh again. Laughter had been a lost commodity in my life for so many years.

The knight soon captivated all our hearts with his charm. Nearing my final laps, he managed to ask if I would have dinner with him later that night.

I was not prepared for this.

He must have heard the hesitation in my voice when I nervously responded, "I don't think I can tonight. I have a busy day tomorrow."

The knight decided to find my friend Marilyn. Perhaps she could persuade me to have dinner with him. She would later tell me what he said. "I would really like to learn more about this lady and what she does. She's an interesting person." His words assured Marilyn that he was okay, and she convinced me that this dinner was what I needed.

Reluctantly, I said, "Okay, but I must be home early to prepare for my upcoming fundraising project."

Marilyn and the kids were so excited they came home with me after my run. Marilyn wanted to help me get dressed for my "date." The children were also the "safety team" for their teacher.

Anxiously peering out the window for his car, they were ecstatic when he drove in my driveway.

The kids eagerly welcomed him in.

Thus began a night I would never forget.

Dinner went well; we were the last customers in the restaurant. We drove around town and checked out different venues for my upcoming fundraising project. I also learned that my knight was an amazing salesman who sold products I used in the day care.

During the evening, I finally learned his name. "Happy, or just Hap," he said.

Hap was both helpful and knowledgeable. As the night waned, the more we talked, the more I liked being with him.

Before we finally said good night, we decided we would stay in contact whenever he was in town on business.

Phone calls and occasional visits continued. According to Hap, he had a double purpose to see me more often.

My fundraising event and selling me merchandise for my day care were of great interest to him. I must admit I was happy whenever we spent time together, and according to him, these were his happiest days also.

Thanks to his efforts, our fundraising event was successful, raising thousands of dollars for the MS Foundation. Both the children and I loved the day care tee shirts from his company. With such powerful charisma and humorous stories, it was hard not to want to be with him more and more.

But then there were other times.

My "happy" friend became withdrawn at times. There was little conversation at the track. I began to wonder which guy would show up—Hap or Grump. On occasion, I asked if something was wrong. At other times, I asked if *I* had done something wrong.

His answer was always the same—a terse "I'm okay. Don't want to talk about it."

Now I was really concerned.

Curiosity about his unusual behavior piqued my interest and led me to enroll in a Psychology 101 class at the University of Kentucky. Before enrolling in the class, I met with my professor to discuss why I was interested in this program.

The professor was quick to inform me that there was a name for this disorder, manic depression, and denial was often the reaction of a patient to it.

He agreed to help me start a case study to better understand the disorder's behaviors. Better yet, he decided the case study could be used for my class credit.

I worked on the case study for a full year. The research gave me a better understanding of what Hap was going through. What I didn't realize then was how much my study would benefit me in my future career.

Considering I was training for another upcoming marathon, I was at the track every night for my two-hour run.

Hap was working nearby and would usually show up at the track as well. At least I hoped he would.

Eagerly I watched for him.

His charm had captivated my heart. Yet I moved cautiously to trust this man.

Being loved and appreciated had been missing emotions from my young adult life for many years. Was I ready to trust again?

When he finally showed up, we ran side by side.

Tonight, I would be the one asking the questions. My pounding feet were keeping pace with my accelerated heartbeat. I managed to keep my breathing synchronized enough to bring up my most crucial concern. "What is your marital status?" I asked.

His response was an unflinching one. "I am divorced." He'd already told me that at our first meeting on the track, and he'd also told Marilyn.

Again I accepted his answer, even though I still had little essential information about his background or family history. The only things I was sure of were the names of his ex-wife and daughter.

The Moment of Truth

It was the next day, while on business in the area, he dropped by my house to make a phone call. During the conversation, I overheard him give his phone number to a client. At that time, I still didn't have it. I only knew my knight as Hap—no last name and the town where he lived. I recorded his number in my memory bank until later and wrote it on a notepad.

What was intended as an innocent phone call to his number led to a total wipeout of my emotions. Hap lost his shining armor with that phone call.

Instead of his voice when I called, the voice of a young girl greeted me. When I asked her name, I realized she was his daughter. The only truth so far.

When I asked to speak to her dad, she yelled, "Mom, it's someone on the phone to speak to Dad."

Mom yelled back, "He's in the shower. Take a number for him to call back."

You'd better believe, I did not leave my phone number, and I also ignored every phone call from him later.

Curiosity must have overcome him. This brought him to my house for an "emergency" visit. Involved in the day care, I did not have the time or the desire to talk with him. Three hours later, it became apparent he was not leaving until he learned what was going on.

Finally, I agreed.

Big mistake.

We went to the local coffee shop and situated ourselves in a private corner. As soon as he learned about my phone call with his daughter, he immediately realized there would be some "splaining" to do. He went into a full-blown explanation of the situation at his house.

This should be good, I thought. I mean really good coming from this award-winning salesman.

Nervous but determined to allay my doubts, he reached over and squeezed my hand and continued.

They had been separated for a long time, many months, and he was living upstairs, his wife and daughter downstairs. As Catholics, they were not allowed to divorce. They were dealing with some church issues at this time that had hindered them from moving forward for an annulment.

If this were the truth, then I needed to call his wife, apologize, and explain to her what had happened.

I called.

After sincerely trying to tell her how sorry I was, I explained I would not be seeing him again.

She immediately thanked me but was adamant it wasn't necessary. She said their marriage had been over for a long time, and she didn't want him back in their lives. As in every divorce, there is always another side that needs to be heard, but I accepted her response to my apology.

As the number one salesperson in his company, he was accustomed to winning awards for his performance. The encounter on the running track was another outstanding award-winning performance of his sales ability, and I was to be his trophy.

Longing for approval like many women, I was eager to accept his explanation, yet my instincts screamed that I should turn and run in the other direction as fast as possible.

The Holy Spirit's voice was to "let go."

My heart was enamored. He filled the emptiness within. I was smitten by his charm. When one is driven by emotions of the heart, it is easy to dismiss God's voice inside and make unwise decisions.

As was our custom, we were at the track, but this night, his pace was different as was his humor. "I've got something to tell you." His eyes were cloudy as I glanced at them.

"What is it?"

He took a deep breath. "My company just told me it's transferring me to Houston."

"Oh," was all I could say. I waited for the next statement. Would it involve me?

"I don't want to leave you," he said. "I can't stand the idea of being apart from you."

So I waited for something—a "but" followed by "I'm not going to take the job." An invitation to join him. But neither came. I buoyed up my feelings. I would not allow another man to hurt me. When we reached our cars, I said goodbye before the tears fell.

After that, things changed. He was no longer at the track to run with me and talk about our day. My knight wasn't fighting for me. We had been just talking about our life together a few days ago, and then he was gone, possibly out of my life forever.

A week later, the invitation came from Texas. He had already moved. "You'll love The Woodlands. It's beautiful, and there's nothing like it."

"What's The Woodlands?"

"How far is The Woodlands from Houston?" I asked

"Fifteen minutes at the most. You'll love it."

Moving Forward

Moving forward, chasing my heart's desire, I bought a house and moved back to Texas, where my life had begun. Hap was or now just mere minutes away from my place, and I was content. After settling into my new home, I stayed physically active with running and biking.

With time on my hands between visits with Hap, I became passionate about two foundations that inspired me to pursue their fundraising events. My love for cycling and running led me to sign up for fundraising bicycle treks and marathons. The American Lung Association and MS Foundation offered two upcoming events.

Both events involved thousands of cyclists. Even though it would be challenging and exhausting, I was ready to train for the treks from Houston to San Antonio and Austin.

Determined to keep my mind, body, and spirit in the best condition possible, I continued training for mini and regular marathons as a daily routine.

Then the bomb fell.

I learned Hap's family had moved with him from Kentucky and was living a short distance from me.

Although clearly aware he was not yet divorced, I had justified continuing our relationship until his marriage could be dissolved by the church. Most of the time when we were together, we argued. He was reluctant to go to church and didn't seem happy most of the time.

Since Hap was reluctant to go to my church, I began attending the Catholic Church with him. In a heartbeat, the parish and the priest accepted me and encouraged me to be a lecturer at mass. My style of reading was not a familiar one to the parish; the Word of God was so precious to me. The priest, as well as many members of the congregation, told me my voice was enthusiastic and inspiring. The parishioners eagerly lined up to shake my hand and thank me after the mass.

Hap seemed irritated by the reception I as a non-Catholic received from the parishioners. He also wasn't fond of the priest; they were both strong-willed. Because of Father Charlie's reaction, it became a challenge whenever the two of them were together.

Confused by Hap's behavior, I determined it was time for me to approach our priest and share our marriage dilemma. Hap agreed, and we asked for an appointment to meet as soon as he was available. To our amazement, Father Charlie could see us in two days.

As anxious as I was, Hap was even more apprehensive. The intent of our meeting was to see if an annulment could be accelerated. I explained the information I had, knowing it usually took years to complete.

Without hesitation, Father Charlie reached on the shelf behind him and handed us a couple of thick forms to complete. One set of forms was for me.

I was quick to explain I didn't want an annulment from my previous marriage. We just needed his guidance to help accelerate the process for Hap.

Father Charlie addressed my concerns about annulments and remarriage in the church. It was a complicated process. It wouldn't be necessary for me to have an annulment, but he would see what he could do to escalate the process for Hap's.

After leaving his office, we walked to the car in silence. I finally asked, "Well, what do you think?"

"I don't believe it," he said.

Astonished at his response, I stopped in the middle of the parking lot, turned, and looked straight at him. "What is it that you have a hard time believing?"

"I never heard of any priest escalating an annulment."

In just ninety days, with a tremendous amount of legwork, Hap's marriage was annulled. Reeling from shock, he and his family couldn't believe what had happened.

The church doesn't move that quickly as his voice resonated with disbelief.

I too did not understand the process. It seemed to depend on the circumstances and the priest. Even though I was not Catholic but a charismatic, born-again Christian, the parish and its priest seemed to respect me.

The major clash of personalities continued between the priest and my husband-to-be. Both men demanded to be in control at the same time. In every issue, they were both always right.

It seemed that many of my values and lifestyle choices were different from Hap's; however, Father Charlie supported my views.

I remained faithful to the values of my Italian Christian heritage taught to me as a young girl. I would not ignore or devalue my self-worth.

A no-shack-up relationship was my requirement.

This award-winning salesman, with all his persuasive talk, thought it was the okay thing to shack up. After all, we were going to get married.

His reasoning made sense to him; it was the reasonable thing to do. His apartment lease would soon be up, and he wanted to move his stuff to my home.

Again he reminded me we would soon be married.

I had not given a lot of thought about moving his belongings into my house, but later I agreed on my terms.

He would have to sell or store what couldn't fit neatly into my home. This agreement was also contingent on our upcoming marriage.

Agreement Accomplished

With the invitations mailed and RSVPs returned, I became excited about our imminent December wedding.

The sun shone brightly through the beautiful stained-glass windows on this day. The magnificent array of red poinsettias appeared even more brilliant.

It had only been a few months earlier that we were concerned if his marriage was to be annulled. All parties also had to agree.

They did.

Today my knight would become my husband.

I was a nervous bride, so much tension building to this day.

Our podiatrist friend Jerry and his wife, Vicki, were our attendants. They helped calm my nervousness with their assurance, reminding me of surviving the struggle. This was the right thing for both of us, they insisted.

Excitement flooded my heart when I looked out over the audience and saw my daddy sitting with his distinguished camera around his neck ready for action. There was a time when he was not in favor of this union and sternly voiced his concern.

Sitting nearby were my Catholic aunts and cousins, who were still reeling in disbelief that an annulment had been granted so quickly to make this day possible. They smiled and gave me a thumbs-up as I walked down the short aisle.

After the brief ceremony, the blessing, and communion, we repeated our vows and then received a final blessing from Father Charlie before he introduced us as husband and wife.

A lovely reception followed in the dining hall, which had been elaborately decorated. The aroma of coffee permeated the air as did the scent of freshly baked goodies. The band was in full swing by the time we entered, and our guests applauded us as a newly married couple.

The Unknown Discovered

It wasn't long into our marriage when I discovered another aspect about my new husband.

A scary discovery.

It made me feel as if I were on a runaway roller-coaster ride. I don't like roller coasters, never did, and I certainly didn't want to take this ride. Up today and down tomorrow.

The charming man who had wooed me, who had swept me off my feet, I later learned was from a dysfunctional family. I suppose that was why he never talked about them, even though I asked him on many occasions.

Eventually, while searching for medical information on his family, I learned his younger brother had committed suicide and his father and grandfather were alcoholics. With this unexpected discovery, it helped me to understand more about his unpredictable behavior.

Month after month with the roller-coaster experience of the emotional ups and downs, there seemed to be more downs than ups.

It became more obvious that Hap's problem was not going to improve without medical intervention.

The search began.

My research this time was on personality disorders and their behaviors. It became clear we needed to discuss the family information I had discovered.

There was hope if he sought help. Hopefully, he was eager to do so.

It was very obvious now that my fun-loving husband had disappeared, and another personality had slipped in and was holding Hap hostage. This man being so filled with rage led to constant marital issues.

Would he be willing to seek medical help, or was this the denial the professor had warned me about?

Total denial.

His refusal to discuss any possibility of seeking medical or professional help bewildered me. This denial later turned to anger, then rage. I had never been exposed to such in my lifetime. If our marriage were to survive, it would require vast amounts of oxygen for us to breathe and to live a normal life. But it required that each of us put on our own oxygen masks first if we were to help each other.

His behavior became increasingly debilitating. Eventually, I considered removing myself from his degrading verbal abuse and living elsewhere. I had never been subjected to verbal abuse in my home as a young girl. Swearing was considered off-limits, especially to a woman.

Devastated, I began my intense quest for help.

The five-year medical journal entries that began in Kentucky from my studies at the university became even more valuable now.

My husband's outrages escalated at the same rate as my search for support. My health and safety were in jeopardy, living with his terrifying outbursts.

Being unaware of what I had done or said to escalate his rage seemed to be the most immediate question I needed an answer for.

The data jumped off the pages as a warning to me. For my safety and well-being I became even more cautious.

Instead, I became more cautious and remained.

A veil of darkness covered each bipolar episode. Each month, as his cycle approached the downward spiral, he would sleep longer. He required that the bedroom and family room drapes be drawn all day.

I maintained this lifestyle for many years.

Four days into his spiral-down time, I knew not to discuss any issues or ask for any input about our business.

Most often, the caregiver can also become codependent in the relationship and blame themselves. Codependent individuals seem to think that they are needed by the other person, and they in turn need to be needed.

Eventually, one starts to think if they just tried harder, their partner wouldn't be suffering as much.

As codependent caregivers we tend to take the blame for the partner's behavioral issues. Without healthy boundaries, we can take on unnecessary guilt.

My bipolar husband constantly reminded me I was the one who needed professional help.

And I did.

I did not know how to cope with such a riveting lifestyle.

Professional guidance and help kept my self-esteem levels full and functional.

A Professional Challenge

Making matters more challenging, we were both motivational speakers and our company offered leadership and management training seminars.

My husband was extremely powerful in his work and always expected perfection from himself. Considering he was ADD and bipolar, Hap was his own worst enemy. I was his number one fan. There were times, however, when his behavior was so overwhelming I would have to step up and complete his seminars.

One such occasion came at the conclusion of a three-day seminar in San Antonio. The company had prepared a beautiful affair to honor him. His presentations had been outstanding.

After packing his materials, he came up to the hotel room, took a shower, closed all the drapes, and turned all the lights off.

No amount of persuasion regarding the importance of this event at eight o'clock moved him toward the door. He insisted I go and tell them he was just too tired. It became my responsibility to make excuses to the hosts.

With sighs of disappointments, our hosts knew how hard he'd worked and were pleased that I attended the celebration since I was also part of the team.

The plane ride home the next day was also a challenge. He chose to have breakfast alone and without me.

He refused to check us out of the hotel and left for the airport alone.

I had been left with all the luggage and equipment.

Later when I learned he was already at the airport, I had to decide how to transport myself, the equipment, and the luggage for my return home.

When I arrived at the airport, I explained to the flight attendants my dilemma.

They had a plan.

I waited until after he had boarded the plane; then just before the door closed, they seated me in first class. He would have departed the plane had he seen me on board. His plan was to leave me stranded in San Antonio.

And thus the downward spiral of his suicidal behavior began once we were home.

*****

Life for Hap became an even bigger challenge, one he didn't feel he could handle.

Busying myself with errands and office responsibilities, I removed myself from his space while he was in this dark, spiraling-down time.

It was the following beautiful Saturday afternoon.

I became concerned when I continued to call home from my luncheon date with my girlfriends. The phone kept going to voice mail.

I called his buddy Rocky. "Would you do me a favor please? Hap is home and not answering the phone. Would you drive over and check on him and see if everything's okay?"

Rocky immediately agreed.

After he rang the front door with no response, he went to the back door to check on him.

There was no response to his knocking.

Rocky decided to check the garage to see if his Mercedes was there.

As he approached the garage, he immediately smelled an odor coming from underneath the closed garage door.

As he heard the motor running, he raced to the garage opener, raised the garage door, and found Hap sitting behind the steering wheel staring at him.

Rocky yanked open the door.

"What are you doing?"

"What does it look like?"

As Rocky struggled to shut the motor off, he noticed the stuffed tailpipe.

Dragging Hap out of the front seat to the outside patio, Rocky began his questioning.

"Hap, what are you doing? What were you thinking?"

Again, Hap replied, "What does it look like?"

I was in the kitchen at Rocky's house with Helen, his wife, when he brought Hap to a safe place to talk.

We all tried to bring Hap back to reality.

Nothing worked.

Rocky suggested he take him to the clubhouse. He could shower and use the whirlpool and steam room. Hopefully bring him back to reality.

Two hours later, Rocky brought him back to their house.

While we were sitting around the table eating snacks, Hap left. We thought he was in the theatre room watching TV.

Hap had disappeared out a side door and was a "runaway."

Now what were we to do? Which way did he go?

Should we call the police for backup?

Rocky drove his little sports car down the busy highway looking for his buddy; I headed in the opposite direction.

Driving slowly, we combed the area looking for a wandering suicidal man.

Rocky spotted him first. He was walking by the highway.

He drove up beside him and got out of his car, but Hap refused to get in.

I arrived shortly after Rocky had called me for help from his cell phone. I should mention his phone was not a smartphone; it was a big box, one of the first on the market. It came in handy because he was able to call for police backup as well.

After a stressful struggle, we finally drove him to the psych hospital.

We both breathed a sigh of relief when the staff greeted us and took him to safety.

This was one of the most difficult tasks I'd ever done.

I had to leave my husband behind locked doors, banging and shouting for me to take him home.

Dr. Rosenthal, the psychiatrist, while doing his entry assessment, was overwhelmed after he learned about my five-year medical journaling regarding my husband's bipolar state.

Obviously, I didn't have the journal with me, but he was excited to know that I had been dedicated in journaling my observation for such an extended period of time.

He asked if I still had my little black book.

When he learned the data were current, he stood, leaned over his desk, and said he would wait if I would get it for him.

Unaware of the reason for his urgent request, I agreed and immediately drove home to retrieve the black book.

Later, I learned the information within it was important for my husband's medical recovery now because it was of his day-to-day behavior.

When I returned, Dr. Rosenthal sat down with me to explain his urgency. It appeared my five years of journaling also affirmed an extensive study that had been in progress to confirm the cause and effect of the bipolar disorder.

As earlier stated, my journaling began when I became aware of Hap's constant pattern of serious downward trends when we were dating.

Not realizing then that these trends would last for approximately the same length of days every month, I learned there is a definite pattern of behavior.

Knowing that I am not the cause of his behavior is a welcome gift of relief.

According to sources of Mayo Clinic, bipolar disorder, also known as manic depression, affects more than 5.7 million American adults in the United States.

This disorder not only affects the family but also causes disruption in the work environment as well as social relationships. In Dr. Rosenthal's review with me, he confirmed that genetics and the environment can alter brain structure and chemistry.

So this was what I was living with each month?

I never knew how the severity of his behavior would be manifested.

In layman's terms, Dr. Rosenthal explained that his chemical imbalance was like that of a woman who suffers from PMS each month. This chemical imbalance is what caused Hap's behavior to spiral each month.

With the doctor's explanation in a language I understood, it gave me more clarity and helped me to remove the self-inflicted guilt for his behavior.

It is such a devastating and demoralizing experience for a codependent caregiver to endure.

There is so much more help available today. With advanced research, no one need suffer alone in shame.

As a codependent caregiver, my first desire was to help my husband get better. I thought if I tried harder and made better choices, he would improve.

What I learned while in counseling as a recovering codependent, I am not responsible for his behavior or his recovery.

Recovering Codependent

If this is your introduction to the world of bipolar, or if you're living with a person with the disorder, there is hope. My bipolar ride was filled with my husband's erratic behaviors and many disappointments.

Living with one painful experience after another can be overwhelming.

I invite you to ride along with me and hopefully learn from my experiences—a journey from the perspective of the caregiver.

The Bipolar Ride

From time to time, my husband refused to take his meds. For whatever reason, eventually, he would go into a downward spiral.

Before one of his downward spirals in March, we had a two-week window of time free of seminars.

We both needed this time for a much-needed break. The only problem, so did the entire college and high school communities in the country.

March is not a good time to look for accommodations in warm areas of beaches and sunshine as my husband had requested.

Leaving solo for his last seminar before our break, he insisted I arrange for those accommodations when he returned from his trip.

Despite the aid of two travel agencies, it wasn't going to happen. If they found a location near a beach, no flights were available. If they found air flights available, there were no hotels available.

The exhausting search came to an end when I discovered a lovely resort/spa with great amenities in Utah.

It was advertised as an amazing place for relaxation.

Who couldn't relax with massages, lavish spas, walking paths, and a challenging bike trail? All the meals prepared with a healthy approach in a most serene area of the country.

I was excited.

This sounded perfect. I was sure he would be just as excited, I assured myself.

While unpacking his suitcase, I sat on the edge of our king-size bed, anxious to tell him and see his reaction to our great Utah getaway.

I should have known better.

Not only did he not share my enthusiasm, but he also became hostile.

I rounded the other side of the bed to explain.

Nothing was available, I tried with confidence to relate to him. All flights were full, and hotels near beaches not available.

He became belligerent that I hadn't followed his request. Explaining the situation only escalated his rage.

He refused to listen and stormed off to the kitchen. I followed with my Day-Timer calendar in hand to show him the itinerary.

He stopped in the doorway, turned, stared into my bewildered eyes and shouted, "I'm not going."

My voice then escalated as I informed him about the five-hundred-dollar nonrefundable deposit.

This meant absolutely nothing to him. He was determined he was not going.

After retrieving my calendar from him, my voice returned to a normal pitch. Even though I trembled in disbelief, I spoke up. "If you choose not to go, I will go alone."

He became angrier, began swearing, and said, "If you go, I will divorce you."

After giving him a twenty-two second thought, I positioned myself in front of his hostile glare. I extended my right hand and responded, "Can we shake on that?"

We did, and I went alone.

This was a scary experience for me.

To be bold and not allow his behavior to affect my choice was nerve-racking.

Facing My Fears Alone

Flying to Las Vegas alone, renting a car, and driving through unfamiliar territory to a resort I had only read about in an ad was a challenge.

I was not disappointed.

It was a beautiful, serene resort. I enjoyed every precious moment for seven days. There wasn't any bipolar behavior to interrupt my time of fun and relaxation. Spas, massages, beautiful walking and bike paths. And of course, the healthy prepared meals by Chef Lorraine were outstanding.

The beauty of Utah was country I had never seen before. I experienced it all alone and happy.

The resort was so kind to apply the deposit for both of us to my stay. In fact, they worked hard to ensure my visit would be memorable after they learned of my situation at home.

But all good things eventually come to an end.

Back to the War Zone

Unsure of what conflict awaited me when I returned home, I'd soon find out after the DC-9 landed.

Back to the war zone.

I raised the shade to let the noon-day sun in so I could capture my thoughts before landing. The landing gears began to lower, ready to touch down into enemy territory.

Soon the doors would open for me to deplane.

My steps were slow and uncertain as I walked toward the baggage claim area.

When I spotted the nearest phone, I raced to call our secretary for my transportation home. After I gave her my arrival information, she said she would meet me soon at "passenger pickup."

Shortly after our phone call, she had me paged. She wasn't allowed to come and pick me up.

Not allowed?

My husband, her boss, informed her she would be fired if she did.

I was stranded.

A kind transportation driver of a "reservations only" van overheard my conversation. He immediately came over as I stood by the dangling phone I had dropped.

He offered to drive the twenty-five-mile trip home at no cost to me. He assured me he would get me home safely. I guess he saw my tears and assured me that everything would be okay. With a sympathetic smile, he retrieved my luggage from the baggage carousel.

After pulling into my driveway, the young man grabbed all my bags and we headed to my front door.

There we encountered my bipolar husband's behavior. He had locked me out of my house with the alarm set and no key for me.

The young driver remained on the porch with my suitcases in hand and said he wasn't leaving until I was safe.

Once again, I had to use my big-girl voice and be fearless with my husband. With the courage of a mighty army, I marched up to the window where he could see and hear me and yelled with a firm voice. "I will give you exactly two minutes to open the door before I break a window."

The alarm would sound if I broke the window, and the police would show up.

In thirty seconds or less, the door opened.

Hap could not afford another encounter with the police.

After tucking a generous tip in his jacket pocket, I thanked my dedicated driver for his kindness and concern for my safety.

He praised me for not backing down from a hostile situation. "Ma'am, I'm sorry you were treated so badly."

Darkest Days Yet to Come

My confusion intensified with his digressing behavior. I was trying desperately to grasp the many whys.

Why were the curtains drawn and the room darkened during the day?

Why was he sleeping most of the day with no personal care?

Why wouldn't he attend a client party given in his honor?

Why wouldn't he honor our confirmed travel plans with family?

My whys soon turned to suspicion.

Why were there so many unusual mysterious phone calls?

Why would he avoid most conversations with me?

It wasn't long before I observed his calls were longer and in a quiet voice of secrecy.

Then the calls continued behind closed doors.

When I addressed my suspicions that his conversations appeared to be romantic, he became angry with me.

Christmas was approaching, and it had never been a favorite holiday for him, but I began gathering all the Christmas decorations to decorate our home.

Hap became hostile and refused to let me decorate; I protested. Not even a tree?

My suspicions were on high alert now.

He wanted to change our Christmas plans to meet up with our friends in New Orleans.

He decided he was going to New Orleans without me.

Of course his erratic behavior wasn't a surprise to me, but what would our friends think if he went without me?

Did bipolar behavior ever make sense? So far it had not.

My gift of intuition helped me put the pieces of the puzzle in its proper position.

Remembering all those secretive phone calls behind closed doors could be the missing link to why I wouldn't be celebrating Christmas in New Orleans with our friends.

Later, I learned my husband and his former girlfriend had planned the trip for some time with our friends in New Orleans.

I probably missed my calling; I should have been a detective.

Not knowing the name of the hotel we were to stay, I searched through some files on my desk and located our reservations.

I called the hotel and asked to be connected to our room.

Who do you suppose answered the phone?

Our friend George.

After he recovered from the shock of hearing my voice, he struggled for words when I asked if I could speak to my husband.

In a quivering voice, he yelled, "Timmy [his real name], the phone is for you!"

A series of unprintable words followed before he answered the phone. There were more questions than conversation from his end.

How did I know where he was? Why would I be calling him?

My response was as kind as possible: "Well, you are my husband, and I'm just checking in to see if you're having a good time."

There was long silence before he finally hung up.

Now he and our friends realized I was aware of what was going on. Sometimes, the more you know and the less you reveal makes you stronger, and your opponent weaker. They can become fearful of unknown knowledge.

Now What?

She was not just any girlfriend, but the mother of their son conceived while in high school. Because of the rules of the Catholic Church, as a teenager he was never allowed to see his son and she was in a home for unwedded mothers.

His son was twenty-one before he ever met him.

With his bipolar guilt-ridden mind from high school days and his disturbed girlfriend, he imagined they could go back decades and make life happen differently.

The New Orleans affaire continued.

I chose to spend time with my family in Kentucky for Christmas and not be alone.

After returning home, I was shocked beyond disbelief that he brought her to our home. They slept in our bed, and she decorated our home with the Christmas trimmings I was not allowed to touch.

Our Christmas plans became their Christmas plans. He had reunited with his lost love in New Orleans. For me it appeared the end of our marriage was near. My rocky roller-coaster marriage with a bipolar man would soon disintegrate into another statistic. Was this another marriage failure?

His goal for now was an unknown future of fantasy—to live happily ever after with the white picket fence and the roaring fireplace.

With little trust remaining, I struggled with the thought of another divorce. I was no match for a bipolar husband, who refused to take his meds as prescribed by his doctors.

My husband lived with many years of losses and guilt from his past and crucial mistakes he had made. His father, a fireman, died in a house fire. His only brother committed suicide, and he was not allowed to be a father to his own son. His first marriage had failed, and he lost his father-daughter relationship from that marriage.

Hap's long-distance relationship with his high school girlfriend extinguished any chance for our marriage.

As soon as he could be free, he wanted to marry the "woman of his dreams," the mother of his son from decades past. Moving back to Pittsburgh was his "happily ever after."

I'm not sure why, but for some reason, there was no remorse from me when he chose to leave.

I helped pack the clothes he wanted to take. But there were three remaining closets full of new clothes with tags still attached. Whenever he was in a manic mode, he would buy shirts, shoes, suits, and accessories he never wore. Rarely was I allowed to go shopping for what I needed without an argument, but his manic conscience was assuaged once by buying me a blouse.

It was a real challenge to cram all his personal belongings into his newly purchased Toyota. My husband always said I had a black belt in packing. I could pack the most in the least amount of space. I filled every available area with as much as I possibly could.

Genuine peace flooded my heart as I closed the door, making sure nothing fell out.

In his thinking, he would soon be on his way to absolute happiness with no problems.

Early the next morning, we met at a nearby restaurant for breakfast before his long drive to Pittsburgh. Standing in the parking lot, I said my final adios.

After he started his car, he rolled down his window.

"If this doesn't work out for me, I hope your life won't be so complicated that I can't come back."

With the quickness of a bolt of lightning, with his window still down, I declared my feelings of pity for him and a heart of gratitude for me.

My parting words to him: "As soon as you drive out of this parking lot, don't look over your shoulder or even think of coming back. I will never take you back."

Never?

And off he drove.

Not Over Yet

Sometimes, life can throw us a curveball when we least expect it. I certainly wasn't ready for mine. I was out even before getting up to bat.

According to the divorce terms, the house must be sold and all profits divided. In a short time, we had an offer on the sale with earnest money. The realtor mailed all the documents to Hap in Pittsburgh for his signature. His new lady friend received the documents but *forgot* to give his mail to him.

Sometime later while working at the Houston Open, I happened to see our realtor also working at the Open. When I asked her how much longer before the closing, the shocked look on her face informed me something was terribly wrong.

"Did you not receive the mail I've been sending you?"

I was oblivious to what she was talking about. That was when I learned the documents had been sent to Pittsburgh.

I was unaware of the urgency, and the signed documents had not been returned.

The offer expired, and we lost our home in foreclosure to the bank. Not only had I lost my husband to his high school sweetheart, but I also lost my home.

Psalm 103:6 says, "The Lord works righteousness and justice for all the oppressed."

Determined to pick up the pieces of my shattered marriage, I knew I must find new beginnings and move forward after another failed marriage.

I would not be defeated. I might be down, but I was not out.

Fully aware God was in control of my life, I knew he was able to make it even bigger and better than before.

Vince Lombardi's "Winners never quit, and quitters never win" was my new motto. I identified myself as a winner and began my search for new direction—new adventures with God, who never left my side.

I was shocked when I learned my bipolar husband had carefully and secretively removed my name from all joint funds.

He left me with no income.

I became aware of this after I tried writing a check for groceries from our checking account.

Why would he do this?

I was a vital part of our company, and our joint income went to pay our bills and provide money for Hap to splurge when in his manic mode.

How would I continue to live?

The only money he had no control of was nine hundred dollars I had received from my father's inheritance.

Nine hundred dollars was not much, but when given to God, it could be multiplied. *With God, all things are possible.* If Jesus could take two fish and five rolls and feed at least ten thousand people, he would provide for me as well.

I asked God for guidance on how to invest my nine hundred dollars wisely.

Crazy Idea and Amazing Miracle

What happened next was an amazing miracle.

I decided to open a unique gourmet sandwich shop with my loaves and fishes.

"That's a crazy idea," my family and friends said. "Nobody starts any kind of business with only nine hundred dollars." They were sincerely concerned that I had lost my mind.

I was recognized as a good negotiator, and it appeared to be an asset to help lease the building I would need as the first step in establishing the Gourmet's DeLite.

After explaining to the landlord I only had nine hundred dollars and faith in God, he agreed to give me three months' rent-free until I could begin operation. He was quick to remind me the restaurant enterprise was a difficult endeavor, but he liked my concept and determination and would be willing to work with me.

Now that I had the building, I also needed a good chef and equipment.

I approached Jerry, a chef at the country club, and asked if he would be interested in helping me in a start-up operation.

Jerry was ecstatic about my idea of offering gourmet sandwiches and soups. He'd always wanted to work independently and to be more creative with his talents.

But what would he say when I told him there would be no compensation until we had a cash flow?

His enthusiasm never waned. "I will do whatever it takes to make this successful."

I offered free room and board for him and Bucky, his Lab retriever.

With Jerry's knowledge and enthusiasm, we began going to auctions and shopping for used kitchen equipment, dining tables, and chairs.

We printed our menu items and posted them in the window. After distributing menus to offices and stores in our immediate area, we were ready to open.

Nervously we placed our "Open" sign in the window.

Would they come?

How would we handle the situation if there was a crowd?

How would we handle it if there wasn't?

Dan and Jerry, my first helpers in The Gourmet's Delite

Opening Day

Our nerves were soon put to rest.

To our amazement, all eight tables filled rapidly with hungry, enthusiastic customers. The excitement was contagious for the guests who filled the room. Every seat was filled. Laughter and high fives permeated every inch of the place.

Wow. What a challenge.

Would we be able to continue to serve everyone our magnificent, healthy fare? My son Dan helped when available.

Since the customers were on their lunch break, we needed to move quickly to serve everyone properly and in a timely manner.

Quick was the goal.

Our wonderful customers even picked up their waiting orders, grabbed their drinks, and even wrote their own receipts. Most paid with cash to expedite the process.

In tears, I stepped back and marveled at this enthusiastic lunch crowd who did what I was unable to do. They did so with laughter and appreciation for our little eatery.

Word travelled quickly throughout the business community. The Gourmet's DeLite became the place to go, and one review even read, "It's worth the wait, and to clean your own table."

In a few months of soup and sandwiches served six days a week, one of our loyal customers suggested something different.

"Since you're Italian and known for your lasagna, and you have your chef to help, why don't you serve lasagna one night a week?"

Jerry and I discussed it and agreed it was a good suggestion. We would make lasagna and serve it with salad and garlic bread one night a week.

The closest authentic Italian restaurant was in Houston. We'd have a captive audience in The Woodlands.

We posted "lasagna night" in the window. It read, "Lasagna Tonight—6:00 to 9:00 (or as long as available)."

I'm not sure if it was a good idea for just me and Jerry and my son Dan as needed.

We had to buy more 16 × 20 baking pans because the two pans of lasagna we used sold out in the first hour. Most customers called ahead for reservations—not for one of our eight tables but to reserve their order of lasagna so it wouldn't be sold out by the time they arrived.

With the overwhelming aroma of the garlic bread and lasagna baking in the oven, the line stretched into the parking lot. It was *beyond all thinking*.

Customers were aware that if they had a table, they would have to clean and set it up for their dinner.

Still they came.

A billionaire business man by the name of George Mitchell approached us one night. George and his wife, Cynthia, loved good authentic Italian food and asked me to consider moving our facilities into larger quarters.

Isaiah 54:2 says, "Enlarge the place of thy tent, and let them stretch forth the curtains of thine habitations: spare not, lengthen thy cords, and strengthen thy stakes." In the NLT version, Isaiah 54:2 says, "Enlarge your house; build an addition, spread out your home, and spare no expense."

From that scared, recently deserted, divorced woman with nine hundred dollars in her pocket who dared to open a sandwich shop, now I was being approached to "enlarge the place of my tent." The God I know, love, and serve has never let me down or misdirected me!

George and Cynthia Mitchell wanted to elevate my little sandwich shop to an upscale Italian restaurant, complete with a full menu of my Italian favorites and a full menu of fine wines.

They drove weekly to Houston for their Italian cuisine but wanted to invest in my restaurant for authentic Italian closer to home.

Scoma's Italian restaurant of The Woodlands came into existence after much prayer and consultation with the Mitchells.

Cynthia's decorators' and gardeners' work was unbelievable. The interior dining facility became a masterpiece of serene beauty with twenty-five tables.

The luscious patio with its ten tables and twinkling lights had an area for a band nestled among the fountains and clinging greenery.

Nothing was lacking in this restaurant. It was first class all the way.

Jerry helped plan our extensive menu, but the specialty of the house was my lasagna. With a select staff of servers, busboys, and kitchen help for Jerry, we were almost ready for the grand opening.

If we wanted returning customers, two things really mattered: quality service and food.

We must have done a great job with both because the waiting line each night to get a table in Scoma's Restaurant was a long one. The amazing aroma of garlic and the freshly baked bread made standing in line worth the wait.

This picturesque setting had a constant flow of traffic driving slowly past our restaurant listening to the band and observing the dancing crowd on the patio.

A common occurrence for our "regulars" were the hugs and kisses from me before being seated. If I were in the kitchen or with other customers, they would say to the maître d', "We will wait until she is available."

My hugs were an authentic Italian form of greeting designed to make people feel welcome.

Beauty from ashes. From a humble gourmet sandwich to unknown new beginnings, God restored what had been taken from me.

This powerful billionaire and his wife, who miraculously appeared in my life, made sure I was successful.

Scoma's of The Woodlands became known for quality, authentic Italian cuisine. Many of our customers drove in from Houston.

"What Satan meant for evil, God used for good." After what Hap did to me, this couple's generosity, love, and support were *beyond all thinking.* Scoma's Restaurant was just the beginning of many prosperous ventures together.

After completing their regular six o'clock Monday evening dinner, George and Cynthia asked if I could join them to discuss an "idea."

An investor had approached them to purchase the building where Scoma's was located. We would have to evacuate but not for a while. George was quick to allay the concern in my eyes. He said that this was the time to relocate me into whatever business I wanted.

George was the founder of Mitchell Energy and developer of The Woodlands, also known to be a caring person to anyone he could help.

Concerned for my future, George proposed several options if I didn't want to continue in the restaurant industry.

As much as I had loved my years as a restauranteur, I longed to return to my first loves—speaking and training.

George liked my idea and asked if I would train his 360 managers, staff, and employees who worked in his hotels and restaurants. Subject matter: customer service.

This assignment would be extensive, but I'd have as much time as needed to complete it. George decided that since I lived in The Woodlands and would work in Galveston with all of his properties, I should not make the daily drive. He and Cynthia made provision for me to own a condo on the Galveston Seawall.

The daily seminars with management and staff members combined for an extensive training program on making George's operations more customer friendly.

This was quite a stretch for me to do solo since Hap and I did seminars as a team, but now I was on my own and used my training abilities to motivate this very energetic group.

Like a spy, I went undercover as a customer in many hotel and restaurant properties. I listened closely to the staff's phone responses at the hotels' front desks. I pretended to be an irate customer and posed complaints or demanded an immediate remedy. Then I evaluated the staff member or the manager's response and handling of the problem. Of course, each manager was different, so I made room for different styles of managing customers and guests.

My spy work proved invaluable in targeting my seminars to reach problems without pointing fingers at individuals. Managers learned how to treat their employees the way each needed to be treated. Morale rose to new heights.

I evaluated restaurant and hotel employees on their greeting at the entrance, the length of time before the server appeared, and the quality of food and service. This was part of the training experience of the various properties.

Living in Galveston provided a new lifestyle for me.

I loved condo living, sea breezes, and long walks along the seawall. However, my training season was about to end, and the Mitchells were adamant I should not leave the island. I had a home in the Hill Country and in The Woodlands, but neither location was suited for another business opportunity if I wanted to be employed.

Cynthia invited me for lunch at one of our favorite restaurants. After our entrée had been served, in her gracious, soft-spoken voice, she leaned forward and said she had an idea for me.

Of course, I listened.

One of her projects, close to her heart in Galveston, was Sa'saparilla's, an old-fashioned ice cream parlor. Cynthia described the history of Sa'saparilla's and how it would be the perfect place for me.

"I'm not really interested in going back into the restaurant business," I said.

Cynthia's sweet and persuasive manner assured me an old-fashioned ice cream parlor would be nothing compared with operating an Italian restaurant.

My Angels, George and Cynthia Mitchell

She continued how the entire mahogany decor in the parlor was shipped from an old saloon from another country. Included in the decor was an antique player piano. This parlor was used for movie scenes and birthday celebrations around the old piano.

Sa'saparilla's on The Strand soon became another adventure in my life of unknowns.

In addition to the thirty-one flavors of hand-dipped ice cream and specialty ice cream desserts, we introduced our wonderful brownies and specialty coffee bar.

The permeating aroma of brownies baking and coffee brewing brought passersby inside to grab a hot brownie and a specialty coffee. We served the $1.50 slices wrapped in tissues directly from the pan into the waiting hands of the customers. As quickly as they were cooled, we had to make a new batch.

It soon became necessary to change the process. Customers had to take a number as they waited in line for the next batch of hot brownies. Yet there never seemed to be a complaint from those in line.

My sweet Cynthia was ecstatic that the business was thriving with lines out the door in the place she loved so much. And George—well, he just stood in line and read the *Wall Street Journal* while waiting for his double-dip cone. No freebies for him; he was adamant about paying.

Galveston became home for many years.

God, George, and Cynthia Mitchell transformed my entire life *beyond all thinking.*

*****

Cynthia and her twin, Pamela, were identical, and I do mean identical. On several occasions at the mailbox, I would engage in conversation with Pamela, thinking I was talking to Cynthia.

She'd smile and say, "I bet you think I'm Cynthia." The girls were so close they even married in a double-wedding ceremony by an army chaplain in 1943.

George and Cynthia's amazing family began with a great boom in 1945, when their first child was born. It let up in 1963 after the tenth child was born. They were known among their family as the circle ten. I loved being around this family and admired the children's love and respect for their parents.

The Tremont House was another of Cynthia's real loves. It was also one of the places where I celebrated my sixtieth birthday with Cynthia's attentiveness. For two days we celebrated.

A Mardi Gras marching band of guests paraded from the Tremont House to Sa'saparilla's for the grand finale, tooting horns and throwing beads. This grand lady and George made this an unforgettable celebration.

My sweet Cynthia was eighty-seven when she passed away in 2009. The entire city of Galveston honored her with the greatest of memories. It was Monday, January 4, 2010, when my sister-in-law, Alice, and I drove to Galveston to be part of Cynthia's memorial service. The church was standing room only. After the service, there was a beautiful procession led by bagpipers to the Tremont House. George rode alongside in his little scooter.

George was ninety-four when he passed away at his home in Galveston in 2013. Among his many visionary accomplishments, he will forever be remembered as the father of fracking, a unique real estate developer, and a philanthropist.

He was also the developer in 1974 of a unique community known as The Woodlands, where I lived. Every detail was planned with an eye toward the environment, from how parking lots were positioned to how rainwater ran off each yard.

With his passion for trees, George made a nuisance of himself among the construction crew, reminding them to leave as many trees as possible in a 28,000-acre development thirty miles north of Houston. He loved living among nature, which reminded him of his early childhood. No building could be built taller than the tallest pine.

Environmentalists and developers criticized his ideas. They said, "He doesn't know what he's doing. After all, he's a successful oil man, not a real estate developer." The son of an illiterate immigrant,

George didn't inherit his oil fortune. He was unpretentious and even a little shy in social settings but was also known as a man with a caring heart for people in need. He specialized in doing things no one else did—in energy, real estate development, and historic preservation. George disregarded the status quo with a vision that brought him beyond his greatest dreams.

He left a legacy for Texas.

Both George and Cynthia Mitchell will be remembered forever as my best friends. My brother Steve penned these words on his note to them: "Thanks for being our sister's guardian angel."

Lessons Learned

When you seem to lose everything and you feel like a failure, God is still in the boat with you during the storm, and he will never forsake you.

What goals and ambitions have you laid aside because you lost faith in people and maybe even in God?

What positive things are you telling yourself?

Negative?

God sends angels to help us in our darkest moments.

He loves us; we're his kids.

Remember, *when you do the right thing for the right reason, you will get the right result.*

Whom do you need to forgive that mistreated or hurt you deeply?

Write it down and forgive them so you can move forward.

Live today free of anger and hostility.

You deserve a better life.

CHAPTER 7

❦

Back to Dating

Now that my hectic work schedule was settling down, I decided it was time to enter the dating scene.

After joining a dating site, I was unprepared for the overwhelming interest from men looking for a relationship with a Christian lady.

The men I met were nice gentlemen who knew my beliefs before meeting. Despite my high expectations as a Christian lady, I was inundated with dates from four states and even London. My social calendar was overflowing. The most exhaustive problem: I had too many marriage proposals.

Stan, an older gentleman in Dallas, was determined he was going to marry me "whatever it took." I wasn't interested in marriage and did nothing to encourage his thinking, but he insisted he would change my mind.

A comment he made was a cause of my concern: "If you throw enough money at a given situation, it can become yours."

A short time later, with a $35,000 custom diamond ring for my finger and an unhealthy amount of determination, he was sure I would eventually say yes.

Stan wanted to make me happy since I'd been so unfairly treated in my previous marriage. With my happiness in mind, he made a trip alone to the courthouse without my awareness.

On one of my visits to Dallas, Stan informed me he had been to the courthouse and proudly waved a marriage license in front of me. He was quick to suggest we go to Florida for the wedding.

Each time we were together, our conversations morphed into a battle of the wills.

Stan made every day a little more difficult until I agreed to the Florida trip.

I knew I would have the support of my son and his wife, who lived in Florida, to intervene if need be.

Thinking he had won the battle, he gloated like a puffed-up rooster. All the while, I knew there was not going to be a wedding, now or ever. Even if a marriage to Stan could bring me anything my heart wanted, the price was unacceptable for my self-respect.

After we'd had a lovely dinner with my family, Stan asked my son for my hand in marriage. It was obvious to my son I did not want to marry this man, but Stan wasn't taking no for an answer.

My son replied, "That will have to be her decision." That was not what he wanted to hear.

After our return home from dinner, my family suggested it was safe to tell him, "There is not going to be a wedding," even with that magnificent diamond.

The next morning while sitting beside the indoor pool, I pulled a chair beside him and explained again I was not in love with him, although I enjoyed being with him.

There was not going to be a wedding.

"I cannot marry you."

It did not go well.

Just as I had expected, he became irate.

No words were spoken from this point on between us. He immediately called the limo service for our flight back to Dallas.

I packed my bags for the painful flight home.

Not a word was said, but the tension was loud and clear during the forty-five-minute drive to the airport.

After arriving at the airport, he changed our seats on the plane. This was a good thing for me because I dreaded the flight home.

It was going to be difficult when we arrived in Dallas, but I prepared for the worst.

My car was parked at his home, which meant I had to go there to pick it up.

After arriving at his house, I put my bags in my car, retrieved my belongings from inside, and headed to my Hill Country home, where peace and quiet awaited.

The Unexpected Phone Call

An unexpected phone call from Pittsburgh interrupted my peaceful week. The voice on the other end sounded familiar with a tinge of nerves.

It was Hap.

Hap said he needed to talk with me about some unfinished business regarding our marriage.

A decade later?

He asked if I would meet with him if he flew in from Pittsburgh.

For certain, there was never closure to our ten-year marriage. Any damage he caused was now under control after he'd left me penniless.

My plate was full now and a bit complicated. Stan was still pursuing a marriage with me even after the Florida episode. I wasn't sure how to give him the beautiful diamond back without a scene.

And now more drama from the past?

God had been gracious to me. I thought that I should at least be gracious and allow him to come to Texas.

Fully aware (from her lover girlfriend, who called often) of him and his wife's present living condition and all their bad experiences, I said I would have to think about it.

She was living a double life with him and her lover girlfriend. They had major fights, and he'd been evicted from their home on numerous occasions.

Not sure what to do or say, I told him I would pray about it.

I did.

God spoke to my heart and gave me peace it would be okay.

There would be healing for both of us from the wounds of that painful marriage.

One Month Later

The three-hour drive to Houston Hobby Airport brought a new awareness: I was afraid of the unknown.

What kind of behavior should I expect after ten years? Would I even recognize him?

I arrived an hour early. Still afraid of the unknown, I wasn't sure if I was doing the right thing even after God had given me the okay. I could turn around and go back home and leave him stranded or do the right thing. By this time, I wasn't sure what the right thing was.

My mind drifted back to the dark days of our marriage. I immediately remembered the poem I wrote when he left me in that parking lot early in the morning, his brand-new Toyota packed for Pittsburgh.

Today, he was flying back to Texas.

Today Is the Day!

One of God's greatest gifts to us
Is the ability to remember and to forget.
Remember the good, the pure, and the fun,
Forgetting those things that would hinder the run.
There's no use looking back on that which is done.
Look forward... Be happy... Today has begun.

Finally, I parked my car and headed toward the terminal in search of a prodigal man. Wasted life, wasted years, ready to make amends.

My head held high and my shoulders straight, I walked with confidence toward the baggage claim area. I wasn't sure if I would even recognize him.

I observed every male crossing my path. They all seemed to look alike, but there had to be some way to identify him.

I was nervous now because almost everyone had deplaned. He should be looking for me also, so that should help.

Was that him in the distance looking a little lost? When he tugged on his pants from the back to pull them up, I was almost sure that was Hap.

I approached slowly, then stopped, a little uncertain.

When my courage renewed, I stepped in front of this man, extended my hand, and called him by name.

When his eyes connected with mine, I wasn't prepared for what happened next. He grabbed me, pulled me toward himself, and holding me in his arms, said, "Oh my god, is this what I left?"

Visibly trembling now, I was not sure what would happen next. Was this the same man who left me?

Why was he so surprised that I looked so young and happy? I had changed after ten years.

So had he. He was about forty pounds heavier.

The other passengers hurried to claim their bags, but he stood staring at me, saying how beautiful I was. What had he expected to see? A sad and lonely woman? His eyes traveled over every part of me, and he noticed the rock on my left hand. With a confused look, he asked, "What is that?"

With all the noise of the conveyor belt dropping bags and the chatter of anxious and excited passengers, I tried to explain about the gentleman who was in pursuit of marrying me.

"Oh," he said as he dropped my hand to my side. And for the first time, a glint of disappointment showed in his eyes. I was wondering if he was recalling his last words to me before driving out of the parking lot headed to Pittsburgh.

"If this doesn't work out, I hope your life won't be so complicated and I can come back."

We continued toward the baggage claim area.

After claiming his bags, I noticed he became a little uneasy. There would be so much to talk about on the three-hour drive home. Hopefully, he would be more at ease.

I reminded him while making the three-hour journey to my home of our earlier phone conversation; he would be my guest and would be occupying the guest room while here.

I hoped to find out soon why he was so anxious to see me after ten years. Also, I hoped I'd hear an apology to put some closure to his abrupt end of our marriage. All the lies and deceitful situations he became involved in. That was all I needed or wanted from him.

His parting words echoed in my ears also even after ten years. And yes, I remember my reply to him. "Never."

Sometimes the winding Texas Hill Country roads at night could become a real challenge because of the deer. I had to stay alert, hoping my headlights would capture their movement on the side of the road. Driving was much easier at full moon since deer tend to sleep during that time.

We took a break and stopped at a popular restaurant for dinner after driving an hour out of Houston. This allowed us time to visit in a more relaxed environment. The food was as good as usual, but the conversation was information gathering for me and reminiscing for him.

After dessert and coffee, the two-hour stop helped, and I was ready to complete the drive home. His job was to help watch for the deer.

Exhausted from the drive and the airport experience, I was glad to drive into the carport. It was awkward for me as we walked up the twenty-two steps to my condo door. After I put the key in the door, a smile appeared as I was reminded this was all mine.

We continued down the hallway to the guest room for him to put his bags down. He was amazed as I gave him a tour of my condo with all its beautiful decor.

Sleep was not on either of our agendas. We had so many lost years to retrieve, so much pain that needed healing. I still remember the lingering feelings I felt at the airport when we saw each other for the first time when he grabbed and hugged me. It felt natural to be in his arms again, yes, even after all the painful things he did to me in the past.

The next morning after a sleepless night, I was still listening intently to his many apologies even though I was exhausted.

Then he did something that confused me. He walked toward where I was sitting and pulled me close, kissed me, and told me what a fool he had been to ever let me go. I wasn't ready for what my body felt in that moment.

During the three days together, I was grateful to hear him acknowledge what a sick man he had been, and he finally was seeking help to be "normal" again.

The three-hour trip back to the airport was less stressful. For the first time after the tumultuous years of our divorce, I had closure after a decade of separation. Information can be good, but explained information can bring more resolution. Detailed information during our visit was what I needed with the truth.

He explained that the goal of the woman with whom he'd betrayed our marriage was twofold. She wanted to get even for her past as a pregnant teenager, and the other was to get his name. After ten years of marriage, and with his name, she was ready to divorce him. She was eligible now to receive his Social Security.

She did just that, although she only lived with him for five years, was separated for five, and then divorced him when the time was right for her.

One Year Later

Two of my girlfriends had recently experienced broken relationships, one a marriage. I invited them to come to my Galveston condo for the day for a let-it-go party.

We were going to get rid of our past hurts together. The day was well planned. I had yellow legal pads for each of us to write letters to the guys who had hurt us. We sat in silence on the floor for hours pondering the exact words to write. It was a solemn and emotional time.

After we penned the final words, it was time for the ceremony.

We placed our letters in plastic zipper bags and carried them across the street to the beach. Our project continued as we searched for rocks and shells to weight our bags; then we proceeded to the final phase. We headed to the end of the jetty.

First, we stood in a circle, held hands, sang a song, and said a prayer over each bag. Then with a mighty thrust, each of us tossed our sealed bag filled with the rocks, shells, and the letter chronicling our past hurts into the sea. We cheered like a seventh-grade pep squad as we watched each bag float out of sight, and disappear by the mighty waves.

Except for mine.

For some reason, when it came my turn to hurl my bag, it refused to float away. This confused us.

Why wouldn't it float away like the other two?

We grabbed fishing poles from nearby to poke at my bag, but it refused to disappear like the others. With my camera in hand, I captured a picture of the reluctant bag that lingered by the dock.

A collage of pictures captured from that day hangs on my wall as a constant reminder of Hap's bag refusing to disappear.

Later that evening, still confused why mine refused to float, I wrote this poem:

Letting Go

What do you want from me, dear God? I asked
What will it take to be whole at last?
It's so awesome to feel your touch, warmth, and love
When I sit in your lap for our wonderful chats.
"I have wonder, excitement, and love in store for you,
Release all your fears and give them to me.
Letting go, my child, is not as hard as it seems.
Give them all to me and then you will see."
With my bag filled with rocks, all my hurts and my pain,
I tossed them out to the sea for the waves to carry away.
Today is the day I let go of the past.
There's no turning back; there's peace at last!
Thank you, Father, for courage to stand firm and true
I thank you for a new destiny, too!
December 5, 1993

I didn't realize until I added the date at the bottom of my poem that our little ceremony happened on our wedding day.

I know the plans I have for you.

After our reconnection reunion and his divorce finalized, our communication continued as did frequent visits. Hints of romance started to evolve. I was not interested; I still had a diamond ring that needed to be returned to a man determined to marry me.

As determined as Stan was to marry me, I was as determined to return that beautiful customized ring in its original box. I made the trip to Dallas with a sense of fear. How would he react with this final rejection?

My normal procedure to enter his house was through the garage door entry. How would I enter today? Should I knock as a guest?

Contemplating what to do, to my surprise, Stan met me at the door and invited me in. As he led the way through to the sitting area, I was in for the shocking surprise of my life.

"Let me introduce you to my fiancée."

Fiancée?

"Well, I guess congratulations are in order? When's the big day?" I asked.

"This coming weekend."

Still in shock and trembling as well, I reached into my bag to retrieve *the ring*.

With the ring in my grasp, I walked toward Stan and his lady and handed the ring to him; and to my absolute disbelief, he turned and slipped the ring on his new lady's finger.

On my drive back home, I thought how he must have "thrown enough money to get whatever he wanted." That was Stan's philosophy.

Looking in my rearview mirror as I drove away, I smiled and thought, *I'm priceless.*

*****

The phone calls from Pittsburgh continued with more visits. Vivid memories reminded me of our past, and I wasn't interested in a repeat performance.

However, one day when I least expected an interruption in my life, God spoke to my heart and said *I was to marry Hap again.*

Do what?

This couldn't be God talking to me; it had to be the devil. I buried the thought.

Until one day, while in prayer, it became very real to me. It *was* God speaking to my heart.

I did not want to think about marriage. But God became specific with every detail. "I want you to marry him again because in his old age, he will not have anyone to care for him except you."

At the time none of this made any sense to me.

Why me?

I was only aware of the present. He had a mother, sister, son, daughter, and grandson.

"God, if this is what *you* want me to do, then I will do it as unto you." I continued in prayer that day.

Still in disbelief that God would ask this of me, how could I tell my caring family?

After all they suffered through that marriage and his affaire and betrayal. This was one of the hardest decisions of my life. I didn't want to hurt them, nor did I want to fail in my promise to God.

Days and then months of reestablishing our relationship, the reality of marriage was on the horizon. Still unsure of announcing this decision to my many friends and family, I struggled with reality.

Finally, in desperation of doing the right thing, we set a date, yes, another December wedding day for us.

December 10, decades later after our first marriage. A judge friend of mine performed the ceremony in the home of another friend. Simple and special but with no celebration from family or other friends.

We were married for six months before I finally decided the best way to announce to my family and friends we were married again.

My big seventieth birthday was in the horizon, and as usual for our family, a big celebration was going to happen.

This would be the perfect venue to announce our marriage. This special event was also going to be a family reunion.

Not a better occasion to make my announcement surrounded by so many family members.

So how did I make the announcement?

At each guest seat, there would be a personalized coffee mug filled with goodies. One side of the mug would read as follows:

Jo Ann Scoma
Happy birthday!
70
August 27, 2005

The other side of the mug would read as follows:

The McElroys
Tim & Jo Ann
Congratulations!
Dec 10, 2004

With bated breath, I waited for my guests' response and how long it would take for them to get the messages.

As each person began to remove the items from their coffee mug, they saw the greetings, and then their first reaction was shock.

After the shock, and looks of disbelief, some clapped and cheered, and others cried.

Emotions were mixed.

Was this a day of celebration, or was this the advent of a repeat performance?

I understood their concerns probably more than they were aware. What they didn't know was I considered this a mission more than a marriage.

The first three years of marriage were in part healthy and somewhat normal. It was never picture-perfect, but I was pleased with the happiness we enjoyed despite our past.

God had chosen me to complete a plan he had for Hap. This path, unknown at the time, would lead to his suffering and disability.

My Mission Begins

I wasn't sure what it meant when the doctor diagnosed my husband with Parkinson's disease. My niece, a neurologist, suggested he be examined when we returned home from a family gathering. She had noticed some signs of the disease and wanted it verified by doctors in Pittsburgh.

After extensive testing, the medical staff was sure of their diagnosis. They explained every detail and answered most of my questions about a disease I knew nothing about. I understood the painful diagnosis but wasn't ready for their last words.

"There is no cure."

After his first diagnosis of the disease, during the next seven years, we experienced an overwhelming change in his quality of life. At one time, Hap was a handsome college quarterback and a successful businessman who enjoyed a lavish lifestyle. Now it was heartbreaking to watch him struggle to do everyday tasks.

Depending on caregivers to assist with his eating and bathroom tasks was humiliating for him. No longer even able to pull up his pants, he required constant care.

God knew fifteen years earlier this day would come when I had questioned him that Hap had a family who could take care of him.

Not me.

But where was his family now?

His sister and mother had both passed away.

For many years, he had been estranged from his only daughter.

His son was available only when I called for assistance. Hap was not allowed to stay in his home because it caused problems.

The promise I had made to God was real now.

His constant care was beginning to take its toll on me both physically and emotionally. I was counseling full-time, managing our home, and caring for him almost nonstop until the end.

He expressed to me numerous times how he was only existing, not living.

Hap also was aware of the toll it was taking on me. He would say, "I just don't know how you do all you do."

I always answered him with the same response.

"I'm doing what I promised God."

Return from Nashville to Final Respite Care

With Hap in respite care, I was returning home from my yearly conference in Nashville with plans to stop in for a quick visit before going home from the airport drive.

It was so dark and there was a terrible rainstorm I was unable to safely drive to his respite care facility. I called from my car and told him that Emmy, our little Maltese, and I would be there tomorrow.

His anticipated cigar box from Nashville filled with miniature moon pies would have to wait until then. It was too dangerous to continue driving in such a storm.

Emmy and I arrived at the care center the next day late in the afternoon. We planned to have dinner with Hap and then an extended visit. But it was not to be.

Hap was adamant we leave and soon.

I was shocked and then terrified.

"What's going on?" I asked with my amiss mind.

I tried explaining I had to gather his laundry and tidy up his room before going to the day care the following day. The bus was scheduled to pick him up in the morning for day care, and then the bus would bring him home in the afternoon.

"I'm not going home!"

His eyes were fixed; his voice was loud and demanding.

"Get a big brown box," he demanded. "Put all my clothes in it."

When I asked where he planned to put it, he bellowed, "I don't know, but you must pack them up." Then to my dismay, he ordered me and Emmy to leave immediately.

Confused, I continued packing up his room, explaining he would be coming home the next day.

His voice became even louder, filled with intense anger. He shouted, "I'm not coming home! You must leave now."

I finished gathering up all his dirty clothes and personal items. A staff member helped take them to my car. Reluctantly, we said a final good night and left our kisses on his brow.

It was early the next morning at 3:54 a.m. when I received the shocking call from the center. "Mrs. McElroy, your husband has passed away."

I insisted this could not be true because I was just with him, but with their affirmation, I told them I would call them back shortly.

Immediately I called Janice the hospice nurse and told her about the phone call. Like me, she did not believe it to be true either.

"Dr. J, I was just with Hap today and spent several hours with him laughing and telling jokes. There did not appear to be any signs of immediate pain or death."

"You wait and I will check it out. There must be a mistake. I will call you back."

She did and it was true. My husband took his transition to heaven. Without a struggle, he was presently in the arms of Jesus.

So many unfinished conversations about my trip. His cigar box of moon pies.

Life is like a vapor, here today and gone tomorrow.
My husband was only seventy-five years old when he left us.
Without regrets, I kept my promise to God.

Lessons Learned

My purpose for writing this book is to bring hope to the despairing person.

Never to give up.

No matter how bleak your situation is or how much injustice has come your way, never say never.

A thought to remember: *little is much if God is in it!*

The events that took place in this chapter are *beyond all thinking*.

The unbelievable events eventually led to a life of purpose. We don't have to understand why God asks us to do certain things; we just need to remember he knows the plans for our lives. Obedience to his prompts is essential, even if they seem unreasonable as God's instructions to marry Hap again were to me.

What lessons did you learn from my journeys in this chapter?

Has God ever prompted you to do something you didn't want to do?

How did you respond?

CHAPTER 8

Beyond All Thinking: At Any Age

From my early childhood, Daddy was my inspiration when it came to challenges and competition.

He instilled in me this lesson: if I wanted something of value bad enough, I could make it happen if I persisted.

I'm sure that is why I am still so competitive with myself and others. This does not mean I always make smart choices.

It was on a beautiful Saturday morning. I was about eight or nine at my cousin OM's house. My siblings and cousins challenged me to stand on my head on the trapeze.

The trapeze hung high in the big oak tree in his front yard.

Of course, I accepted the challenge.

I was the oldest of all the cousins and siblings and a girl; I had a lot to prove. I didn't disappoint them with that feat.

But they wanted more. This time, I wasn't allowed to use my hands as I balanced on my head.

I did it.

I had evidence to prove it several hours later as I left the emergency room with my despairing parents.

My right arm was broken in six places, and I had to wear a cast with a sling for many months in the hot Texas summertime. I wore my autographed sling with honor for my friends but not for my parents.

When I was eleven, Daddy entered me in a sack-hop race event at a Sears family outing. The event was for the employee 's children; the prize was a twenty-five-dollar war bond.

The pressures of competing with all the big kids did not alarm me, even though I was small for my age.

There was never a thought of losing in this event or disappointing my family. My daddy and I practiced every night whenever he came home from work.

His words of affirmation resonated in my heart. "Sister, to be a winner, you must stay focused on what you're doing, and don't look at what the other kids are doing. Stay focused on the finish line and you'll be the winner."

I was a proud little girl as my family cheered me on to victory from the crowded sidelines. The pain of the struggle seemed to vanish in the sweetness of a job well done.

I won the twenty-five-dollar war bond and made my daddy and family proud.

Lesson Learned

Accomplishing life's struggles, *beyond all thinking*, is so much easier if we have self-confidence and others cheering us on.

Sometimes we must make our choices alone.

The more obstacles, the greater the victories.

If God is our constant companion, we are never alone.

What obstacles do you need to overcome?

Is the goal worthy of sacrifice?

Do you believe in you?

Believe in *you*.

Fifty-four and Competing

Even when I was fifty-four, I hadn't lost my desire to compete. I began competing for worthy causes. Many times the cause outweighed the pain, practice, and sacrifice.

For six consecutive years, I pedaled my bicycle from Houston to San Antonio and to Austin. The 150-mile ride (192 to be exact) to San Antonio was to raise funds for the American Lung Association.

With my helmet, gloves, biking shorts, and biking shoes, I was ready. I strapped on my helmet and began my first 192-mile endeavor.

It was a typical sultry Texas October day. The year was 1988, and I was on my way for my first fundraising expedition. My family and friends made pledges to contribute to the cause *if* I completed the ride.

Me and Lacy in our first fundraiser

I did almost everything wrong except for having a bike. The day started with tremendous high hopes of completing this ride so I could collect the two thousand dollars pledged for this event.

Lacy, my new bike, was pink. She was cute with her wicker basket on the handlebars and the metal carrier over the back fender. Did I say she had five gears? With such a luxurious bike, I thought I was fully prepared for the long hot trek to San Antonio, Texas.

I guess I looked more like a member of the Beverly Hillbillies than a long-distance cyclist. The wicker basket on my handlebars was fully packed for any emergency. The metal rack over the rear fender was also loaded with all my other gear.

On day 1, I watched the sun rise and I watched the sun go down.

Day 2 was a bit different. My body didn't want to move, much less get out of bed. It was a difficult task to climb back on my bike. My body wasn't cooperating. It refused to bend in bicycle mode. With encouragement from my team, I tried harder.

Finally, it worked.

On day 2 a medical team was riding beside the riders.

As the sun began to set and darkness loomed on the horizon, Spencer, the director for the ride, told everyone patrolling, "Do not try to stop her."

I *had* to finish. I needed to cross the finish line because of the pledged funds.

My main motivation for this ride meant my brothers would double their pledges, but only if I completed the course. They were sure I wouldn't make it.

They were wrong!

Flashing lights from the ambulance riding beside me and flashing lights from the two motorcycle policemen in front of me provided enough light for me to see. Of course, my sag wagon was behind me for moral support. It was enough for me to cross the finish line dead last.

I was the last rider of the two thousand that had completed the course hours before me. As I pedaled across the finish line, I fell off my bike, too weak to go another step.

Finally, I unstrapped my helmet and headed, with assistance, to the waiting bus and other anxious and exhausted bikers.

How did I feel after the two-day journey in the searing Texas heat? I think all moving parts of my body had been seared.

After the three-hour bus ride home, my body molded to the bus seat. It refused to move when the bus stopped in the parking lot for us to step off.

For three days I was in bed, nursing my inadequately prepared body for such a trek.

I did everything wrong.

But I did learn what to do differently for the next fundraising expedition.

And yes, my brothers had to double their donations. The amount of pledges collected was over two thousand dollars for the American Lung Association.

I was grateful for my maiden bike fundraiser. Although my mind was in the right mode at the beginning of the ride, by the end of the ride, my butt was in total disagreement.

After three days of bed rest, I was able to walk again. Before my next trek in three months, I would have to say goodbye to Lacy. All her cuteness would have to be exchanged for a more appropriate bike for the next long-distance ride to Austin, Texas, from Houston.

Lesson Learned

The lighter your load, the more gears on your bike, the easier it is for pedaling. It offers much better speed for long-distance rides.

The long-distance ride of life is much easier when we remove the unnecessary load of worry and all the heavy cares of life.

Our daily life journey will improve with better speed and unnecessary pain and take us more quickly to *a life of purpose.*

What can you remove from the unnecessary load you are carrying?

1.
2.
3.
4.

Change is difficult sometimes, but to move forward is necessary.

New Wheels and Determination

With Lacy sold and my new bike, Mickey, and his fifteen gears, I was ready for my next Century plus trek.

Mickey was a sleek $1,500 racing bike, ready to conquer the Texas Hill Country quest for a cause. To complete my professional look for this ride, of course, I bought new clip-on shoes, gloves, and a matching helmet. I looked more like a jockey at the derby than a cyclist.

The advancement from Lacy to Mickey felt as though I sold a Ford pickup and advanced to a Mercedes 450SL.

If pedaling to Austin, Texas, from Houston sounds like a pedal in the park, it was in the beginning. The picturesque early-morning beauty and the amazing aroma of the fields of Texas bluebonnets provided an indelible image.

Most of the sponsors for this trek were not aware I had new wheels. For this ride, they were much more generous with their pledges, thinking I would be struggling with all the torturous hills with Lacy.

I had hoped this ride would be less of a challenge than the San Antonio ride.

Seriously? Less challenging?

What was I thinking?

Even with Mickey and his fancy fifteen gears, my clip-on shoes, and gloves, I still had to pedal up those steep hills.

These were the real Texas Hill Country hills. Some had me bent over so low pedaling that my nose was touching my knees.

I was anxious and scared when I looked at the speedometer on my bike. Thirty five miles per hour and flying downhill, all the while squeezing the brakes as hard as possible.

What if I blew a tire? Where would I land?

For this ride, I didn't end up the last of the three thousand cyclists. I finished decent even though I was tired and in some pain. The MS Society presented me with a beautiful crystal plaque as the top fundraiser at the rewards ceremony. I presented them with over two thousand dollars for a hopeful cure for the autoimmune disease.

Mickey was good to me. We did many more cross-country treks, raising thousands of dollars for my two favorite organizations. For six consecutive years, I rode until I was sixty-three, then focused more on my other goals.

Biking to Running

Watching the graceful marathon runners cross the finish line exhausted but proud was another dream to accomplish. Someday I would like to run a full marathon. While living in Kentucky in my midforties, I put this dream into action. I bought my first pair of Nike running shoes and began jogging five miles a day. I was sore all the way. The new shoes hurt, and my legs cramped; but with sheer determination, I was eventually running forty miles a week.

All my official running gear and shoes inspired me to train every day, regardless of the weather or how I felt. Struggling just to make the laps around various tracks, I envisioned crossing the finish line of a marathon to a cheering crowd. The thunderous welcome of shouts of praise lingered in my mind long after I had a relaxing shower.

I will run a marathon someday, I repeated to myself while putting my running shoes away for the day.

The Dream Begins with a 5K Race

My first race was the 5K Constitutional Square Road Race. This historical race started in Harrodsburg, Kentucky, and ended in Danville, Kentucky. A few days before the race, I was in the ER in Austin, Texas, diagnosed with walking pneumonia. I was told to get bed rest, and there would be no race anytime soon.

How could I not run this race? I'd run every day for the past week at the University of Texas track.

And I did.

The enthusiastic crowd alongside the road were cheering and handing out water. This was encouraging as I struggled with my breathing on my way to cross the finish line.

No records were broken, but I was a division winner for the forty-to-fifty age-group. At forty-four and recovering from walking pneumonia, I ran past many younger runners sitting on the side of the road, waiting to be picked up. They did not finish, but I did.

My first-place race plaque is displayed in my home today.

Overwhelming excitement from my first victory made the pain of running less painful. I was hooked. I trained every day, ready for another challenge.

Then Comes the Mini

My first mini marathon was in Louisville, Kentucky. This run was only thirteen miles of the twenty-six-mile marathon. But I was getting closer to my dream of the big one.

However, as a forty-seven-year-old mother, the mini marathon was special for me. Approaching the finish line, I could hear the crowds cheering as they waved their flags of victory for all the runners as they crossed the line. This was what I had envisioned while I was training every day.

What I had not envisioned amid the cheering crowd were familiar voices yelling, "Way to go, mother. You can do it!" Although I couldn't see them, I recognized my kids' voices. Voices of my daughter Debbie and her husband, Clay, but where were they? I scanned the enormous crowd of bystanders, searching in the direction of their voices.

Then I spotted them, perched snuggly at the top of a statue in the park. Their voices were my reward for crossing the finish line.

I was so inspired I wanted to start preparing for the big one immediately. This run was an inspiration for my family. Since my first mini, my children, their spouses, and my grandchildren have become great runners. They've been in many competitions since and continue competing in various runs.

Fifty-Five and Still Running

It finally happened.

At fifty-five, and after many months of dedicated training, I registered for my first twenty-six-mile walking marathon in The Woodlands, Texas. I had an incredibly special partner for this race, my podiatrist.

Jerry thought he should walk with me to make sure I had no problems with my feet while covering this long distance. And he did. Every five miles Jerry had me remove my shoes and socks. He would check for blisters or any other problem with my feet. Of course, while I was sitting on the curb with my shoes off, the runners and walkers continued to pass me. The beaming late-morning Texas sun would soon add to my discomfort if I didn't get Jerry to stop checking my feet so often.

My only escape to cross the finish line before the sun went down was to assure him if my feet were in jeopardy, I'd let him check them out.

He agreed.

I had no damaging pain, and I crossed the finish line.

I must admit, after twenty-three miles, I was hoping there would still be someone at the finish line to pick me up *if* I crossed.

In the next few years, I completed two running marathons without Jerry and several minis.

Qualifying for the U.S. National Senior Sports Classic

Official Entry

What's Next?

These feats of biking and running allowed me to qualify for the Senior Olympics at the age of fifty-eight.

My previous years of athletic training and events helped me to qualify for the 1993 United States National Senior Olympics in Baton Rouge, Louisiana.

To qualify, I had to enter local events in Houston and win first, second, or third place in that category in order to be a contestant in an event.

My qualifying events were track and cycling; I won twelve gold medals and two silver in the one-hundred-, two-hundred-, and four-hundred-meter track events and cycling during the entire qualifying period. What an honor to qualify and compete against the best of the best.

For the opening ceremonies in Houston, I was asked to be the keynote speaker. Wow, what an honor!

I stood at attention at my front-row seat, while the various flags approached the stage with a color and honor guard. Following were the massive number of participants with their flags as they walked across the stage. It was such a moving ceremony.

Amazed, I watched some rather old participants walk across the stage. They each had that look of determination of a winner. Some were in their eighties and nineties.

Soon I was introduced as the speaker of the evening.

I was eager to speak to such a lively group of winners.

"Ladies and gentlemen," the host shouted into his microphone, "please help me welcome our speaker tonight JoAnn McElroy with her inspiring 'Winners Do What Others Won't.'"

My mike was turned on and attached to me as I ran up on the stage. The spotlights were blinding, but with a loud and enthusiastic voice, I yelled, "Isn't it great to be a winner? There are no losers in this room tonight." I went on to say that when we were conceived, we won out of over the fifty million sperms fighting to make it—our first victory; now we were here to celebrate our most recent victory.

The emotional speech brought the Senior Olympian audience to their feet with a five-minute standing ovation. Their tears and waving flags brought tears to my eyes. What an awesome climax to the 1993 Senior Olympic ceremony in Houston, Texas.

My involvement in the Senior Olympics gave me a different perspective on life. I was inspired to strive to live a longer, healthier, and more fulfilling life at any age. The entry level for my age-group was fifty-five to sixty. I was fifty-eight. To be counted among those amazing athletes, some in their late eighties and midnineties, made me feel special.

One event, the shot put, was unbelievable. There were three generations involved in this competition. The grandfather was ninety-five, his son seventy-five, and his grandson fifty-five. What an amazing feat for this family as they approached the podium, amid the thunderous applause, to receive their gold medals for each age bracket.

I was not on the winners' platform and did not receive any medals, but I too was a winner to be involved in such an event.

Maybe three generations of other families would be inspired to become involved. They were so supportive of each other and eager for the next competition in a few months.

With such a model of dedication, I too decided to continue competing and searched for the next local competitions. Setting goals for the next event, I would not consider age as a factor either. I later learned many of the contestants were professionals. They travelled the world with training coaches for these events. What an honor just to compete with them.

My sponsor, Cynthia Mitchell of The Woodlands, assured me I was a winner. "Just being invited with your qualifications makes you a winner in my eyes. I'm honored to sponsor you for such an event," she said.

Lessons Learned

I am convinced the more active we are in our younger years, the healthier, happier, and more productive we'll be in our senior years.

To reach greater goals in life, there must first be *desire* and then *determination* to push through the *discipline* of any training.

You may not be involved with the Olympics, but a desire for a healthier and more fulfilled active life.

However, the many wonderful experiences along the way can introduce you to life's unknown and greatest experiences.

We must believe in ourselves and in God.

What are your goals?

Have you ever set your sights on something that seemed impossible?

Did you start and did you stick to it when the going got tough?

Dream large and don't give up.

This perseverance and determination helped me reach other unimaginable goals in my senior years.

Write three goals you would like to accomplish.

1.
2.
3.

They can lead to a life *beyond all thinking*.

CHAPTER 9

✧

Outside of All Comfort Zones

A different kind of challenge began to circulate in my mind.
What would it be like if I chose to step outside of my comfort zone?

I would have to go *beyond all thinking* to pursue the degrees I never had time to complete when I was younger.

Scary and not a good idea at my age!

I had fantasized as a teenager that I was a therapist, helping my friends with their problems. It seemed I was always helping solve problems for everyone when they were in pain or didn't know what to do.

Even my dolls were clients at one time or another.

In the spring of 1978, at forty-three, I enrolled for one semester at the University of Kentucky. My major: psychology. This was a special time for me. My daughter Deanna, who was nineteen, was also a student on the same campus.

Little did I realize thirty-three years after assisting my children with college and putting my husband through seminary that I too would walk across the stage to receive my PhD in clinical Christian counseling at the age of seventy-six.

This endeavor began when I was seventy-two, when most of my friends had already retired or were planning to soon.

Without any encouragement from my family or friends, I was going to have to take this journey without the team spirit of my past years' ventures.

This accomplishment would be no different from any other. Whether I was biking, running, or training for the Olympics, the goal was to cross the finish line. I would have to make this journey happen with a clear vision and sheer determination if I were to cross this more cerebral finish line.

"Mother, do you know how long it's been since you were in school?"

"Do you have any idea how much studying is required to earn a degree?" These were the questions and concerns from my kids.

Counseling was not an unfamiliar assignment; it had been part of my ministry in pastoring churches for many years as well as youth camps and many other venues. However, my qualifications and former training needed to be advanced in order to deal with the complexities of issues I was now confronting. I would need a degree in order to meet the demands of the prevalent issues presently facing counselors.

I knew this was no easy task. I would have to put blinders on like a Kentucky Derby racehorse and go full speed ahead. No time for grazing, only intense training every day to prepare for the big race. A horse's peripheral vision can cause it to run off course. The blinders are necessary to remain focused. I had to train like a racehorse despite the many responsibilities I faced every day with Hap.

Why was it necessary to put the blinders on if I were to finish the race?

My office was busy with a heavy counseling schedule. I also was a full-time caregiver for my husband in his later stages of Parkinson's.

It was not an easy feat to balance all my other responsibilities and stay focused on my four-year goal.

I completed my bachelor of arts in Christian counseling from Calvary Theological Seminary and my master of arts in clinical Christian counseling from Cornerstone University.

The race was not over for this thoroughbred; I was going for "the Run for the Roses": the doctorate.

The Race to the Finish Line Continues

As I continued my pursuit toward an ambitious goal, my husband required more and more care from me, even with the assistance of additional caregivers. The trips to the ER were becoming more frequent, which meant I was spending long nights and days at the hospital.

You could always follow the night-light to find me studying, either preparing for a big test the next day or preparing for my scheduled clients. There was no time to rest. I had to push forward. Luckily, I didn't have to attend on-campus classes with their limited hours.

My online schedule had no boundaries. I could work as late as necessary to complete my assignments. I had to remain focused with the blinders snug around my exhausted face to prevent any distractions.

*****

Academically, I was doing well until I began to work on my dissertation. This was the most daunting requirement for my degree.

I chose to structure my dissertation on struggles and the reasoning behind them. My purpose was to show we needed to die to self to accomplish our life-changing results. I used the early stages and emergence of the butterfly as a metaphor for my research.

Twenty-five thousand words?

That required a lot of research and writing.

When I began to lose heart in going farther with this project, my friend Dr. Amy McNaughton was my angel of encouragement.

I can still hear Amy's soft, encouraging words: "You can do this."

Amy reminded me that 60 percent of the graduate students never receive their doctorate because they don't start or finish their dissertation.

With her relentless encouragement, we did it!

On May 25, 2012, at the age of seventy-six, I walked across the stage to the call of my name, Dr. Jo Ann McElroy.

My "Run for the Roses" was accomplished; I graduated *summa cum laude*. This honor meant I received no grade lower than an A.

An even greater honor was overcoming the thinking of those who did not believe it possible for someone of my age to complete this goal, much less with any kind of honor.

To God be the glory!

CHAPTER 10

—— ❧ ——

Eighty Years the Matriarch: Should We Celebrate?

The festivities had been planned early in the year to celebrate my eightieth birthday in Louisville, Kentucky, with my family. A birthday cruise was to follow a few weeks later. This was a bittersweet time for me since my husband was unable to travel to celebrate this milestone with me and my family.

Would he be able to enjoy the cruise celebration?

My family, as usual, was supportive during this landmark birthday and made my day special. Any family celebration is always a gift whenever I can have my family with me. Sweet memories linger of that lovely restaurant where the celebration took place. A beautiful portrait from Jo my artist friend was presented to me later highlighting the special occasion.

Another Challenge as a Widow

Thirty days later, my husband made his transition from earth to heaven. He would not be on the cruise to celebrate with me.

I too have had to make many transitions. I became a widow without warning.

Yes, my husband had Parkinson's, but his death wasn't imminent when I left for Nashville for my yearly conference. The box of assorted moon pies that he had asked for was never opened.

The early-morning phone call changed my status from married to widow.

I would be alone. No Hap to care for.

In his own way, Hap waited until I returned from my conference to say goodbye to me and Emmy.

He must have known when he asked me not to leave his moon pies with him. Said he wouldn't need them. Asked me to pack up his things in a big box.

I believe God ordained this eightieth birthday celebrations as a gift to me to help soothe the trauma of the past seven years. Before his death, my husband insisted I take the already-planned family and birthday cruise. My family's encouragement made my going easier. It was good to be with family, some of whom I hadn't seen in fifteen years.

I noticed a beautiful and unusual cross hanging in one of the gift shops on an island we visited. Not only could it be in Hap's memory but also a reminder of this special occasion. To protect the fragile cross from any damage, I carried it on board in my small carry-on bag. It arrived home safely and hangs in my kitchen in his memory.

My brother Charles presented the birthday wishes from my seven siblings in their unique voices. He chose two books, one in honor of my counseling and one in memory of my husband.

Appropriately, the books are titled *Innovative Approaches to Counseling* and *Innovative Approaches to Counseling the Sick and Terminally Ill* by Gary R. Collins, PhD.

Each of my siblings wrote a handwritten letter and placed it in a special place in the books. Imagine, the two books had to be sent to four different states to accomplish this feat. The book also contained strategically placed notes of condolence.

My Siblings Unique Birthday Wishes

Read and enjoy their wishes enclosed in each of the books.

Happy Birthday, Sister:
At your age, sometimes all you need is a little
pampering to help you feel better.

Love,
Charles

Happy Birthday, Sis:
You look awesome. Everyone can't believe you've
reached your 80th milestone!
I hope to age as well, and I will feel blessed.

Love you,
Lillian

Happy 80th Birthday, Jo Ann
You've always been an inspiration to me, and for
that I'm blessed.
You've mothered me more than our own mom,
and for that I'm doubly blessed.
I can't imagine my life without you always being
in my corner.
I speak blessings of joy, health, and prosperity
over you...
In the mighty name of Jesus.

Love Always,
Camellia

Happy 80th Birthday,
Jo Ann, you look fantastic and I pray you have
many more years!

Love you,
Sue and Lou

Jo Ann,

Happy 80th Birthday!

I so appreciate the faithfulness you have demonstrated to the family over the years.

You have worn the Family Mantle well. The footprints you left for those of us in the family who followed you in life have been worthy to strive to equal. I'm so glad you are my Big Sister.

Steve

Happy Birthday Jo Ann!

Every time I hit a milestone age, I look up and you are still 15 years ahead of me. Well, you are a remarkable example of aging well. It gives me hope!!

Love you!
Sam and Lorraine

Happy Birthday, Jo

I have been following you for 40 years. When you turned 40, 50, 60, 70, and even 80, I say, "Well it won't be long, and I will experience this special day." Now I only have to wait 7 more years!

I really enjoyed the birthday cruise and all the stories we shared.

I have talked about you to my men at Woodlands (rehab center), many times. You are a great example for anyone to follow. I'm glad you are my older sister and a leader in our family.

Love Always,
Lawrence

CHAPTER 11

———— ❧ ————

Time to Relocate

I t finally happened!
The reality of living alone as a widow and recovering from a heart attack two months after Hap's death was a major concern of my family.

Being separated from my family by a seven hours' distance drive came to a screeching halt with an unexpected phone call.

My son Dan called to share his good news that he and his wife, Karlene, would be moving back to Florida after years of separation because of their jobs. They were finally going back home.

After I congratulated him, Dan's next words took me by surprise. "And you're going too!"

"I am?" *Do what?* My lips quivered. "Why? When? Where?"

Dan was prepared for all my questions and arguments with immediate answers. "We want you to fly to Florida, meet with Karlene and a realtor, and find your home. Karlene and I are buying you a house."

Now that was an opportunity I couldn't refuse. But I knew the offer would also come with many challenges.

How could I move away from my friends, church, and clients? I questioned.

After praying about it, I accepted their generous offer. Soon I flew to Florida in search of my new home.

My emotions were running wild. Could I possibly find as cozy of a house as mine in Pittsburgh? The number one requirement was a porch. Not just a porch but a study and prayer porch.

The ladies had several houses for me to consider when I arrived. When I laid eyes on house number one's beautiful sunroom porch, I was ready to make the move. Everything in my new house was exactly what I wanted and needed. No need to continue the search.

The contract signed, I had thirty days to pack.

There were eighty-three years of memories, an office, and a house and garage full of furnishings from two previous homes. All must be packed and ready for the moving truck in thirty days. *Thirty days?*

The amazing friends I was leaving behind jumped in and tackled the project with me. Bubble Wrap was everywhere as was the mountain of folded boxes waiting their turn to be packed, taped, and identified with different markers.

The only thing we could not pack was my sad heart. I was leaving behind many memories and awesome friendships whom I'd acquired over the past fifteen years.

I reminisced about the day Hap invited me to move to Pittsburgh after our second marriage to each other. I was not employed at this time. Pittsburgh was home for him since his birth, and he was employed by Allegheny County in a special program. He was well established and known, but I would be starting from scratch.

After my move to Pittsburgh, I fell in love with the city, its culture and people. Soon I developed amazing friendships and found a fabulous church.

The most difficult adjustment was the limited days of sunshine. In awe, I watched my neighbors hunched together on their porches scurrying to follow the precious sun's direction and soak up its limited rays.

The move to Florida, the sun, an abundant commodity, would be a welcomed sight. However, it would require major decisions again regarding doctors, dentists, hairdressers, and of course, nail salons. My insurance providers and hospitals would also change. But the most difficult part of the transition, I was leaving my church family and friends behind.

And then there were my clients. How would they adjust? Would my move complicate their progress and make things worse?

This major move of mine was not acceptable for them. They did not want to change therapists.

But God was good. Many of my Pennsylvania clients wanted to continue their sessions with the latest technology: FaceTime.

After a two-week break, I'd be back in sessions with every client. All of them, including clients in other states, remained with me. The only adjustments were time zones.

The Greatest Challenge

Moving day was quickly coming, and I was having a difficult time leaving memories behind as well as stuff that I had to give away because it wouldn't fit in my new house. The thirty days of packing, wrapping, and stacking boxes to the ceiling were finally done. The reserved twenty-six-foot U-Haul truck would arrive tomorrow.

Dan was worried that my "stuff" wouldn't fit in the truck. He asked the four moving men what they thought.

"Not a problem," one of them said.

"Not a problem? Are you sure?" I asked, reminding them the garage was also full. Even my amateur eyes could see that there was no way all my belongings would fit in that truck.

Still they said, "Not a problem."

There was a problem.

Boxes still remained in the house and garage, and the truck was completely full. I understood just enough Spanish to know the movers finally understood. The loading crew got upset when we suggested they would have to repack the truck in order to get the remaining boxes on.

"No!" they shouted. "Our time is over." After the shouting match ended, we still had a house and a garage full of boxes.

After a call to my landlord explaining our dilemma, he allowed us to move everything remaining in the house into the garage until we were able to move it.

Now that could be a problem. Emmy and I had already landed in Florida. Dan was on his way to Florida with my 1994 Toyota Celica in tow.

U-Haul number one arrived with Angelica the Celica and her interior packed with fragile items.

No time to rest. The boxes had to be unloaded and unpacked inside my new home. The overwhelming task of this move was almost more than I could handle. The interior of my beautiful new home was blocked by mountains of cardboard boxes.

The task before me was overwhelming. Where would I go for help? My packing friends were in Pittsburgh.

God, who is always concerned for his children, provided me a miracle just as he had provided a lamb for Abraham. He provided Alan and Debbie, my neighbors from Pittsburgh. Debbie was the sister of my dedicated packer friend Cheryle in Pittsburgh. They just happened to be vacationing at a resort two miles down the street.

How amazing was this? The boxes her sister had so carefully packed in Pittsburgh weeks earlier Debbie unpacked in Florida.

Debbie and Alan hung pictures and mirrors for three days. All this while they were on a vacation. Friends like them don't happen very often. My heart, overwhelmed with their kindness, sought to repay them.

"No way," was their response. They were just doing what Jesus would do. The remaining unpacking was easier to manage for me, Dan, and Karlene.

What were we going to do with the stuff that did not make the first truck delivery? We would need another truck and driver.

Once again, God provided.

A pal of mine had a friend coming to Florida, and he would be happy to drive truck number two with its load of "leftovers." Little did we realize truck number two, the largest available, would be as large as number one. Each truck had a capacity to hold seventy-four hundred pounds.

Surely, I didn't have that much stuff?

But I did.

Truck number two arrived, requiring more space in an already-full carport from truck number one. What an extremely traumatic move this had been for me. I was still adjusting from my husband's death and recovering from my heart attack. It had only been two years.

Starting over again was not a new thing for me. But at eighty-two?

For several months, I attended church with my family in Florida. We later decided the long drive was too difficult for Dan to get to work after church. The new church was only three minutes from our homes, and we all liked it.

Cornerstone Church became our church. We got involved in activities and served in different ministries. I also had counseling facilities available for some of my clients if needed.

What a blessing to be connected to a church again. My husband's disability made it difficult for me to be involved. He could only be left for short periods of time, not long enough to establish connection. And I was just in the beginning days of attending Grace Life Church and becoming involved with counseling some of its parishioners when I made the move but not without my clients on FaceTime.

CHAPTER 12

—— ✍ ——

What's Wrong with Retiring?

M ost working people anticipate reaching their retirement age.
What *is* the best retirement age? For me, the legal age was sixty-five, but the legal age continues to change, at least regarding government benefits. It will be seventy-two for my grandchildren.

Retirement can also be disappointing, even with well-thought-out plans. In all of life's choices, we should always have a plan B if plan A doesn't work. It's the unexpected events that pop up and can change our best-laid plans in the blink of an eye.

Retirement is defined as "leaving one's job. Ceasing to work." This can be due to reaching a certain age or due to a health issue.

Without a purpose in mind, we can become reclusive in our retirement. However, with purpose, retirement can be a time for reaching new and exciting goals as well as relaxation. Many choose to spend precious time with grandchildren, to travel to faraway places, or to sit by the riverbank waiting for the big one.

Age requirements for retirement with a comfortable investment plan can determine how well one will live their dream. The people without purpose or passion are the individuals who quit or withdraw from life.

Statistics show the retirees without purpose rank among those who die early.

An anticipated purpose and years of planning are necessary for this next stage of life. A healthy retirement portfolio without a plan B can only be a dream when a life-threatening disease or an unexpected tragedy occurs.

It's no surprise that investing in one's health is equally as important. It's also essential to develop relationships and maintain friendships in preretirement years to enjoy when time is one's friend.

Plan B Was Necessary

Daddy began his thirty-six-year career with Sears when he was nineteen years old. A student at Crozier Technical High School, he rode his bicycle across Dallas to work. When he retired, Daddy was only fifty-five and the beneficiary of Sears's original retirement benefits. His thirty-six years of investments in stock began when he first started as a stock boy.

Mom and Dad had looked forward to the day of retiring—she from the day care center she owned and loved so much and daddy from Sears. She reared her eight children, with four of them married. Now they were able to travel to their native Italy and other faraway places. However, the bitter pill of disappointment deflated their long-term plans, hopes, and dreams. They did not get to enjoy the luxuries she had dreamed about.

Plan A didn't work out.

Plan B was now on the table. Mom's health issues changed plan A's dreams. They moved from Dallas to Chicago with hopes of better health care to reverse her long-term battle with cancer.

My mother was a courageous woman. She wanted to enjoy her retirement years and see all eight of her children married. Six months before she lost her battle to cancer, she walked down the aisle for the wedding of her youngest child, Camille. Still, her dream to see all eight children married was not completed. Her baby boy Steve married two months after her death.

Dad's investment in a family business and my mother's fight for survival with cancer destroyed most of their Plan A dreams.

Sometimes the unexpected happens in life no matter how well planned. Even though they had goals for their lives after retirement,

God's plan was different. "'For I know the plans I have for you,' says God."

At the young age of fifty-nine, my mother lost her courageous battle to cancer on December 19, 1974.

Investing in one's health with adequate insurance is priceless. Without health, nothing else really matters in retirement. Mom was prepared to die but not ready.

Daddy's desire to pastor and build a church was fulfilled when he later built and pastored for many years the Singing Hills Assembly of God church. He was on staff at Oak Cliff Assembly of God Church in Dallas, the church where I was married and where my children and siblings were dedicated by Brother Noah who also celebrated both parent's funerals. Daddy ministered in various capacities. He was involved in the prison ministry as well as in his work as the senior care pastor.

Later he became the pastor of the Singing Hills Assembly of God church, which he built and pastored for many years.

Daddy married Naomi and was married for eight years when he too fell victim to cancer. He died at sixty-nine, never having fully recovered from financial losses.

If Age Is Just a Number, Now What?

It's my responsibility to determine what I'll do with the number of years that has been allotted me.

It's interesting to observe my family and friends as they mark places and goals off their bucket lists. I love joining in on their quests to fulfill their goals. I watch vicariously from my armchair their descriptive ventures on Facebook. My interest in travel wanes in comparison with my missions list.

My list began when I was seventy-two.

It wasn't a fun experience in the beginning to pursue my goals. Not as exciting as following North Pole adventures, dogsled riding, live salmon watching, or scenic mountain hiking.

While the boomers continue to complete their bucket lists, I continue to observe their travels from my panoramic armchair. More countries and vineyards of the finest wines. I hike alongside them as they wind along mountainous trails. But I continue to stay focused on my Plan B.

My Plan A was focused and time sensitive. Because of the age factor, I wanted and needed to complete my PhD in four years; this was my dream.

The first half of my life was over, and to reach my goal, nothing could distract me if I wanted to reap the benefits of my dreams. No retirement remained in sight for me. My plan A and plan B are in place.

What a euphoric feeling at eighty-four to have achieved so many goals. I'm enjoying a daily bursting calendar filled with weekly counseling clients.

The face-to-face sessions take place in my office, and with modern technology, it allows me to FaceTime my out-of-state clients' sessions as well.

A dream fulfilled.

Now What?

It's the "Now what?" I want to address. These are actual life events, and hopefully avoided, they will not happen in your life. I cannot stress enough the importance to have a plan A and plan B in place for your retirement. It is as important as an evacuation route in case of an emergency.

The Sports-Forced Retirement

My friend Ralph worked for the NHL for thirty-eight years with the training staff. He worked for three teams and won a Stanley Cup with one of them. Ralph worked on three all-star games and was the trainer for Team Canada. Hockey took him to Russia, the Czech Republic, Sweden, Switzerland, and Japan. He was inducted into the Hockey Hall of Fame.

Ralph was never sick or even in the hospital until forced to retire when the team moved to a new city and only took the players. With a forced retirement, his diabetes took over, and it was one doctor after another. He didn't have a plan B in place for retirement. His idea of retirement was no more working days. This was his plans A and B. With his health problems came the steady pile of medical bills. He had no work experience except for hockey. This left only hourly minimum-wage jobs.

The loss of part of his foot meant no standing jobs, so no minimum wage jobs. Ralph was a jovial, kind man without a plan B and with little hope of digging himself and his family out of debt. His wife had just passed the bar exam. She had to put her dreams for law on hold and returned to work as a high school teacher to support the family and help pay the mountain of medical bills. Ralph's health issues became even more complex and debilitating, creating less of a desire for him to want to interact with the world around him.

An underestimated component of retirement is an unexpected illness or life change. Ralph was a great guy, always putting his family first. His lack of training in other fields with no established goals was detrimental. His early and unexpected death at sixty-nine left his family in a serious financial predicament. In Ralph's situation, his love for his job and personal satisfaction created a sense of false security. He didn't have a plan B. Retirees must always assume a what-if situation. It should include another skill. Ralph had no outside interests or hobbies. His life was hockey. The exhilarating days of the cheering crowds were silenced with his death.

Health insurance must be included in one's portfolio for retirement. One accident, disease, or disorder can empty the bank. As can be seen, retirement requires careful financial planning, setting goals, and creating a plan B years before one retires.

Politically Forced Retirement

Let me introduce you to my sweet friend Diane, who was born with cerebral palsy. She worked for Allegheny County in Pittsburgh for thirty-four years and was an outstanding employee. Her disability made it necessary to use a walker or cane.

Diane was beautiful and talented and did her job with great pride. When she was approached to buy two $250 tickets for her boss's cocktail/political party; she declined to do so. Diane was told she would regret not participating. She explained how her husband had lost his job, and they couldn't afford the expense at that time.

Then things changed.

They timed her on how long it took her to go to the bathroom and how much space her walker took up in her office. Later, her boss advised her not to use the walker in the office because it took up too much space, but she could use her cane.

Once again, she was threatened by her boss after refusing to accept his offer to go to his house with him while his wife and kids were out of town. She reminded him she was a married woman and would never cheat on her husband.

He yelled at her, "Don't let the door hit you in the a** on your way out!" Her boss told her if she reported it, no one would believe her.

She did, and he was right.

Diane lost her battle with the Pittsburgh County office after spending thousands of dollars on attorney fees. She was fired at the age of fifty-four. All retirement benefits and health insurance were lost.

There was no plan B or job security; she had to retire on disability benefits.

Plan B is a must even while still working.

Without it, there can be devastating consequences when politically tied to a party. With Diane's situation, neither good work ethics nor disability was considered. Her boss wanted to get rid of "dead wood" from his office. With the lack of ethical management, a woman's job is tenuous at best.

So I wonder, is there such a thing as job security for anyone? Where was the Disability Act?

Without a plan B, Diane suffered humiliation and failure in a political office. She'd been an employee for thirty-four years with a disability. There was little to no hope for a future job at fifty-four. Plan B is a must in the workplace, political or not.

Fortunately, Diane's contagious smile and positive attitude are a blessing to everyone she meets. She continues to be an inspirational blessing to many in her church.

Beyond All Thinking and a Life of Purpose

At the beginning of this book, I shared the story of my life, a life of purpose at different stages. As I end this story, I want to help *you* wherever you might be on your journey.

If you are a boomer (1946–1964), fifty-five to seventy-three years old; Generation X (1965–1980), thirty-nine to fifty-four years old; millennial (1980–1998), twenty-two to thirty-seven; or Silent Generation (1925–1945) like me, God has a plan for your life regardless of age.

Can you identify with any of the following?

- Spender, no savings account, drowning in debt, a $30,000 student loan, or debt-free.
- Your self-worth is determined by what others think about you.
- Your confidence is unshakable?
- In my research, most people on the job in all walks of life tell me their job is not their dream job, and they're living beneath their full potential.
- What about you?
- What is your dream job?
- Is your purpose being fulfilled?
- Do you *know* your purpose?

A Good Steward of Time

Developing the habit of being a good steward, we must also be a good steward of our time. This will require energy and a dedicated effort.

Time is my most precious commodity. It continues to move me forward at a determined pace. When we realize how much wasted time slips away on frivolous activities, it's easier to be a better steward.

Wasted assets can be watching too much TV, too much time spent on social media, even answering e-mails. I have to manage my social time as well. I am on a mission, and so are you if you want to complete your plans A and B in a designated time frame.

If your purpose gets you out of bed every morning, excited to make a difference in your life as well as in others', you're on your way to achievement. Nothing will stagnate your enthusiasm. Figure out what you've always wanted to do; then fill out a calendar with baby steps to reach your goal.

Lessons Learned

A motivational speaker, an ordained minister, a counselor, and a teacher—I've heard all the excuses. I'm too old, too young, too ugly, too sick, and not smart enough. None of these excuses for not naming and reaching your purpose in life have any merit.

If it's true God has numbered your days and has a plan for your life, what will you do to maximize each day?

What lessons of my story motivate you to say, "Yes, I can"?

What goal will make you put the blinders on and go full steam ahead to reach your goal?

Do any of your goals seem impossible? Why? *Life with purpose, even after seventy-five,* can be your purpose, regardless of when you stopped dreaming.

ABOUT THE AUTHOR

2010

From an early age, the writer was different from other girls her age, travelling around the country as a teenage evangelist. Married at eighteen and the mother of four children, she and her husband pastored in four different states. She was the youngest female to be ordained by her denomination at the age of twenty-three. Marriage to a man who didn't think it necessary for him to seek help for their failing marriage was tough, and even tougher as a pastor's wife. They eventually divorced after twenty-five years of marriage.

At forty-three, she and her new husband travelled the country as motivational speakers for sports teams and corporations, but the discovery of her husband's bipolar disorder overwhelmed their marriage. This discovery led her to research the disorder, which engendered a love for psychology. After her husband left her virtually penniless for another woman after ten years of marriage, she opened one successful restaurant after another.

In her fifties and sixties, she took up long-distance cycling to raise funds for MS Society and the American Lung Association. Husband number two came back into her life, and they married again after fifteen years per God's instruction; but life didn't improve. Still, she rose above her circumstances and competed in the Senior Olympics and was their keynote speaker.

While she and her husband later dealt with his Parkinson's disease, she began a PhD program in clinical counseling and graduated *summa cum laude* at the age of seventy-six. In her eighties, she is a full-time Christian counselor. Her story of perseverance is sure to inspire and motivate the reader to dream big beyond all thinking.

Back Row: Sam, Next Row: Steve, Lawrence, Lou, Next
Row: Charles, Camille, JoAnn, Front Row: Lillian

JoAnn and the Four D's: Dan, Darla, Deanna and Debbie

CPSIA information can be obtained
at www.ICGtesting.com
Printed in the USA
JSHW021353260521
15172JS00001B/7